Easy Internet,
Second Edition

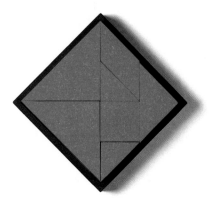

Michael Miller

Easy Internet, Second Edition

Library of Congress Catalog Card Number: 97-65528

International Standard Book Number: 0-7897-1219-9

99 98 97   7 6 5 4 3 2 1

Interpretation of the printing code: The rightmost double-digit number is the year of the book's first printing; the rightmost single-digit number is the number of the book's printing. For example, a printing code of 97-1 shows that this copy of the book was printed during the first printing of the book in 1997.

Screen reproductions in this book were created by means of the program Collage Complete from Inner Media, Inc., Hollis, NH.

Printed in the United States of America

Dedication

To my parents—and their WebTV box, which I gave them for Christmas— for helping me to identify what new users really *want to know.*

Credits

Publisher
Roland Elgey

Publishing Director
Lynn E. Zingraf

Editorial Services Director
Elizabeth Keaffaber

Managing Editor
Michael Cunningham

Director of Marketing
Lynn E. Zingraf

Acquisitions Editor
Martha O'Sullivan

Technical Specialist
Nadeem Muhammed

Product Development Specialist
Henly Wolin

Technical Editor
Alp Berker

Production Editor
Audra Gable

Book Designers
Barbara Kordesh
Ruth Harvey

Cover Designers
Dan Armstrong
Kim Scott

Production Team
Melissa Coffey
Trey Frank
Laura A. Knox
Kaylene Riemen
Julie Searls
Sossity Smith
Lisa Stumpf

Indexer
Sandy Henselmeier

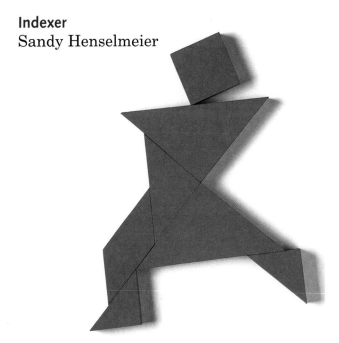

Composed in *Syntax* and *New Century Schoolbook* by Que Corporation

We'd Like to Hear from You!

As part of our continuing effort to produce books of the highest possible quality, Que would like to hear your comments. To stay competitive, we *really* want you, as a computer book reader and user, to let us know what you like or dislike most about this book or other Que products.

You can mail comments, ideas, or suggestions for improving future editions to the address below, or send us a fax at 317-581-4663. For the online inclined, Macmillan Computer Publishing has a forum on CompuServe (type **GO QUEBOOKS** at any prompt) through which our staff and authors are available for questions and comments. The address of our Internet site is **http://www.mcp.com/que** (World Wide Web).

In addition to exploring our forum, please feel free to contact me personally to discuss your opinions of this book: I'm **hwolin** on America Online, and I'm **hwolin@que.mcp.com** on the Internet.

Although we cannot provide general technical support, we're happy to help you resolve problems you encounter related to our books, disks, or other products. If you need such assistance, please contact our Tech Support department at 800-545-5914 ext. 3833.

To order other Que or Macmillan Computer Publishing books or products, please call our Customer Service department at 800-835-3202 ext. 666.

Thanks in advance—your comments will help us to continue publishing the best books available on computer topics in today's market.

Henly Wolin
Product Development Specialist
Que Corporation
201 West 103rd Street
Indianapolis, Indiana 46290
USA

About the Author

Michael Miller is Vice President of Business Strategy for Macmillan Publishing and has been active in the publishing industry for ten years. He is the author of more than a dozen computer books, including Que's *Using Prodigy, Using CompuServe, OOPS! What to Do When Things Go Wrong*, and the previous edition of *Easy Internet*. He writes the monthly column "Miller's View" for the Macmillan Information SuperLibrary newsletter, and he has his own Web pages at **http://www.mcp.com/people/miller/**. His e-mail address is **mmiller@mcp.com**.

Acknowledgments

Thanks to Scott Flanders and the other guys who run the company, for a fun and fulfilling ten years—including the opportunity to write this book and others like it.

Trademarks

Contents

Part V: Nine Ways to Search the Web — 78

Part VI: Nine Web Sites for News and Information — 110

Part VII: Seven Web Sites for Children and Families — 130

Contents

Part XII: Three Things to Know About Chatting on the Net   214

Index   226

Introduction

The Internet has been around for more than twenty-five years, but it is just now becoming a part of everyday life. In fact, it's nearly impossible to read a magazine article or watch a television show without being inundated with e-mail addresses and Web site information.

When I wrote the first edition of *Easy Internet* three short years ago, however, this "mass market" Internet was in its infancy. Most Internet users—and there weren't that many of them back then—were only sending e-mail and participating in newsgroup discussions. The World Wide Web was a relatively new development, and we lacked the sophisticated browsing software we have today. In fact, back in 1994, Netscape wasn't yet a real company, and Microsoft didn't have a single piece of Internet-related software on the market!

Some things haven't changed: The Internet is still a gateway to a multitude of informative and entertaining experiences. From your own personal computer (or WebTV box), you can travel untold numbers of electronic highways and byways, communicating with other computers and users from around the globe.

With today's more advanced technology and the help of *Easy Internet, Second Edition,* you'll be able to:

- Use the World Wide Web to find information on just about any subject imaginable.

- Send electronic mail anywhere on earth.

- Take part in exciting group discussions on any topic imaginable.

- Download just about any type of file you can think of.

- ...and much, much more!

What You'll Learn from This Book

Just look at what you'll learn how to do in this book:

In Part 1, I'll show you four basic things you need to know about the Internet before you make your first connection.

In Part 2, you'll learn about the three ways to connect to the Internet: via an Internet service provider, via a commercial online service (such as America Online), and via WebTV.

In Part 3, you'll discover six ways to surf the Internet: with Netscape Navigator (the browser in the Netscape Communicator suite), with Microsoft's Internet Explorer, with America Online, with The Microsoft Network, with CompuServe Interactive, and with WebTV.

In Part 4, you'll learn how to use Netscape Navigator when I tell you eight things you need to know about Web browsers.

In Part 5, you'll discover how to find things on the Web when I show you nine ways to search the Web.

In Part 6, you'll visit sites like CNN and The Weather Channel as you discover nine Web sites for news and information.

In Part 7, you'll find out how to get your kids online (safely) when you visit seven Web sites for children and families.

In Part 8, you'll learn six other things to do on the Web, including making travel plans, shopping, playing games, creating your own start page, receiving information automatically, and creating your own Web page.

In Part 9, you'll find out how to send and receive electronic mail when you discover six things to know about e-mail.

In Part 10, you'll discover topic-specific online discussion groups when you learn five things to know about UseNet newsgroups.

In Part 11, you'll find out how to find useful computer files on the Internet when you discover three things to know about downloading files.

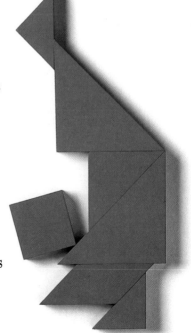

Finally, in Part 12, you'll learn about real-time online conversation when I tell you three things to know about chatting on the Net.

By the way, I've created a special Web page for *Easy Internet, Second Edition*; it's at **http://www.mcp.com/ people/miller/easy2top.htm**. The Web page contains tips and shortcuts you won't find in the book—as well as any post-printing corrections that might need to be made! Also, feel free to contact me via e-mail with any comments or questions; my e-mail address is **mmiller@mcp.com**.

How to Use the Tasks in This Book

I've put together *Easy Internet, Second Edition* in a way that makes it easy to learn all you need to know to use the Internet. Most tasks contain a series of numbered steps, and each step is accompanied by an illustration that shows you how your screen should look. These numbered steps walk you through a specific example so you can learn the task by doing it. In addition, some tasks show you the various parts of a specific Web site (what happens when you click where). For example, if you click where you see the icon "Click 1," you'll be taken to the Web page numbered 1 that appears on the next page of the book.

Big Screen

At the beginning of each task is a large screen shot that shows how the computer screen will look either after you complete the procedure explained in the task or at some point during the task. (Sometimes the big screen highlights an important feature discussed in that task, such as a hypertext link.)

Why would I do this?

Each task includes a brief explanation of why you would benefit from knowing how to accomplish the task.

TASK

54

Responding to E-Mail Messages

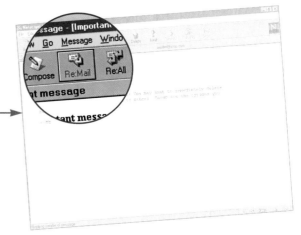

► **"Why would I do this?"**

Many times you will want to send a reply to an e-mail message. In this task, you'll learn how to compose a reply and to automatically send the reply to the sender of the original message.

178

4

Step-by-Step Screens

Most tasks include a screen shot for each step of a procedure. The screen shot shows how the computer screen looks at each step in the process. (Some tasks show the results of clicking on hypertext links on main Web pages.)

Puzzled? Notes

You may find that something went wrong when you were trying to perform a task. The Puzzled? notes tell you how to correct your mistakes and get out of bad situations.

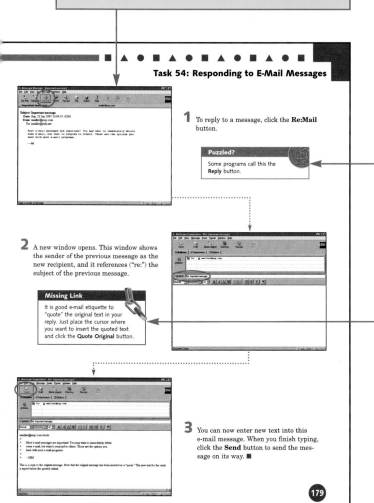

Task 54: Responding to E-Mail Messages

1 To reply to a message, click the **Re:Mail** button.

> **Puzzled?**
> Some programs call this the **Reply** button.

2 A new window opens. This window shows the sender of the previous message as the new recipient, and it references ("re:") the subject of the previous message.

> **Missing Link**
> It is good e-mail etiquette to "quote" the original text in your reply. Just place the cursor where you want to insert the quoted text and click the **Quote Original** button.

Missing Link Notes

Many tasks include Missing Link notes that tell you a little more about certain procedures. These notes define terms, explain other options, refer you to other sections when applicable, give you tips on how to do things more efficiently, and so on.

3 You can now enter new text into this e-mail message. When you finish typing, click the **Send** button to send the message on its way. ∎

179

PART I

Four Basic Things to Know About the Internet

THE INTERNET. YOU'VE HEARD about it. You've seen Internet "addresses" in ads and newspaper articles. You may even have friends who talk about "surfing" the Net. But just what is the Internet—and why would you want to use it?

First off, the Internet is not truly a "thing." You can't touch it, smell it, or buy a box of it. The Internet is nothing tangible at all.

Think of the Internet as if it were a utility, like the electric company. When you hook your house up to the electric company, what happens? Does your house start to glow? Does it spin? Does it sprout a second story? Of course not. When you hook electricity up to your house, *nothing happens at all*.

Nothing happens, that is, until you plug something into a wall socket. You can plug lots of things into your electrical outlets: television sets, radios, vacuum cleaners, blenders—you name it. Only *after* you've plugged in an appliance can you start doing things. When you plug in your blender, you can make milk shakes or daiquiris, it's up to you. The electricity itself doesn't make your milk shake, but because you're hooked up to the electric company, you have the capability to make milk shakes if you want.

The Internet is kind of like the electric company: When you hook your computer up to the Internet, nothing happens. Your computer does not start to glow or spin or grow an extra disk drive. No, nothing happens at all—until you plug in an Internet "appliance." In Internet terms, such an appliance is a piece of *software*, such as Netscape Communicator or Microsoft's Internet Explorer. After you plug in your software, you can use the Internet to do just about anything you can think of, from sending messages to searching for information. All this is possible because you're connected to the Internet.

The Internet itself spans the globe, connecting millions of computers just like yours. This enables you to communicate with computer users in other countries and search for information that may reside on different computers in different areas of the world. And you get to cruise around the world from the safety of your home PC using normal phone lines—and without paying long-distance phone charges!

If you're not yet hooked up to the Internet, this is the section to read first. Here you'll learn these four basic things you need to know about the Internet:

- **How to connect to the Internet—and what to do once you're connected.** The first thing you need to do is establish a connection to the Internet by using your computer, a modem, your phone lines, and an account with an Internet service provider. Once you're connected, you can cruise the World Wide Web, search for information, send and receive electronic mail, engage in special-interest discussion groups, download computer files, and participate in real-time chat sessions.

- **What you need to connect to the Internet.** Is your computer system Internet-ready? Find out everything you need to create a fast connection to the Internet—as well as how to hook up to the Internet through your television set *without* a computer!

- **How to find an Internet service provider.** After you get your personal computer ready, you still need to establish an account with an Internet service provider. Because there are thousands of ISPs across the U.S., choosing a provider is no easy task—but I'll help you narrow down your choices.

- **How to make the Internet safe for kids.** How do you keep your kids safe from unsavory online material? I'll show you how to use such software as SurfWatch and Cyber Patrol to filter out Web sites that contain adult content.

Read these sections *before* you connect to the Internet, and you'll be able to make better decisions about how you connect and what you do when you get connected.

Once you get on the Internet, there are plenty of resources available that show you what you can do and find online. Check out these Web sites, created especially for Internet "newbies":

- A Guide to Cyberspace:
  http://www.hcc.hawaii.edu/guide/www.guide.html

- Global Village's Internet Tour:
  http://www.globalvillage.com/gcweb/tour.html

- Internet 101:
  http://www.sisna.com/users/scotting/101/internet101.html

- Newbie Link:
  http://www.infinet.com/~tmartin/newbie/newbie.htm

- NewbieNet CyberCourse:
  http://www.newbie.net/

And, if you're connecting to the Internet via WebTV, check out the WebTV Tips page at JumpCity—it's designed just for WebTV users!

> **http://www.jumpcity.com/webtv/tipspage.html**

Missing Link

The Internet is an ever-changing medium. Web sites are constantly being revised, and Web browsers are constantly being updated to keep pace with advances in content. Although the screens shown in this book show the most recent version of Web pages and software at the time of printing, what you'll find on the Internet might be different. As folks on the Net say, "ymmv" (your mileage may vary).

How to Connect to the Internet—And What to Do Once You're Connected

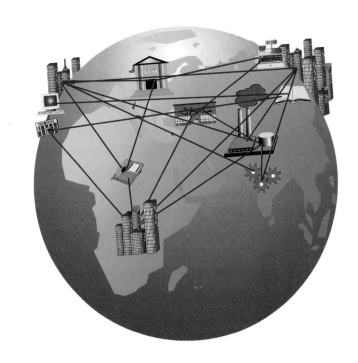

The Internet is really just the means by which a bunch of computers communicate with one another; it's essentially a giant network that connects millions of computers around the world. So when you connect to the Internet, you're connecting your computer to millions of other computers and the information that is stored on all those other computers. This is important, because all the things you can do on the Internet are found on those other computers.

But before you can contact those other computers, you first have to gain access to the Internet. You do this by setting up an agreement with a company that serves as an *Internet service provider* (ISP, for short). An ISP is a company that provides Internet service for you and other consumers. You use the modem on your computer to dial into the ISP, who then plugs you into the Internet via your telephone line. Once you're connected to the Internet, you can start your Internet software (such as Netscape Communicator) and start doing whatever it is you want to do on the Net.

A typical Internet session works like this:

1. You use your computer's modem to dial your Internet service provider.

2. Your ISP verifies that you're who you are (checks your name and password) and connects you to the Internet.

3. You launch the appropriate piece of Internet software, such as Netscape Communicator.

4. You can now send e-mail, download files, or cruise the World Wide Web—whatever it is you want to do online.

5. When you're finished with this particular session, you close your software and disconnect from your ISP, who then closes your current connection to the Internet.

It's *Supposed* to Work That Way...

One more thing about the Internet. You see, it really isn't *managed* by any one person or any organization. Its various parts are only loosely connected, and each site is run independently. Therefore, the Internet doesn't always work the way it should. Sorry, but that's the way it is.

On any given connection, you might find a site that is running slow, is not working right, is not working at all, or is *not there anymore*. Or sometimes the user load bogs down the system, or all the lines to your service provider are busy. Or maybe you won't even be able to connect to your provider for some unknown reason. Or... well, you get the point. So have a little patience if things don't always go as advertised. On the whole, things work more often than they don't.

Things You Can Do on the Internet

After you connect to the Internet, you might wonder just what is there for you to do? Well, when you consider that you now have access to millions of computers—and tens of millions of users—around the world, the sky's the limit! On the next two pages you'll see some of what you can do and find on the Internet.

1 Cruise the wonders of the World Wide Web. The Web is definitely the neatest part of the Internet, where you'll find sites that include graphics, sound, multimedia movies, and hypertext links to other Web sites. You can access hundreds of thousands of Web sites, covering every sort of topic imaginable. See Part 4 for more information about the World Wide Web.

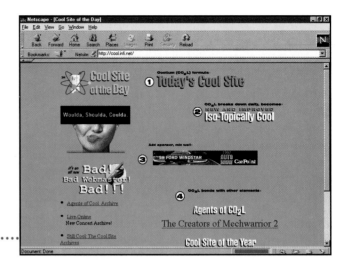

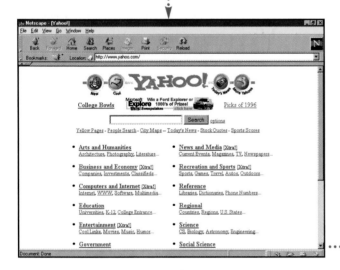

2 *Search for information.* No matter what you're looking for, you can search the hundreds of thousands of computers on the Internet for the information you need using convenient search engines and directories such as Yahoo! and AltaVista. See Part 5 for details on searching the Internet.

3 *Send electronic mail to other users.* The Internet lets you send e-mail to anyone connected to the Net—*instantly.* See Part 9 for more information on e-mail.

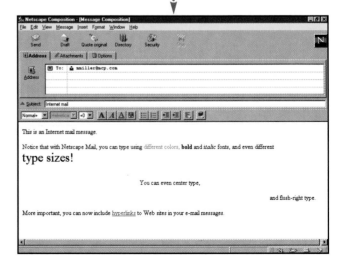

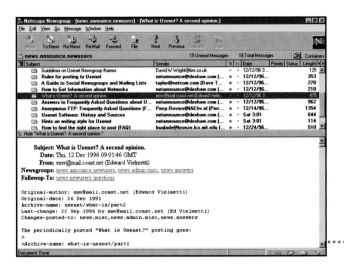

4 *Exchange messages with members of special-interest discussion groups.* You can join literally tens of thousands of special interest mailing lists and newsgroups. Whether your interests include comic books, scuba diving, or biochemistry, chances are you can find a discussion group full of people with similar interests. See Part 10 to learn more about UseNet newsgroups.

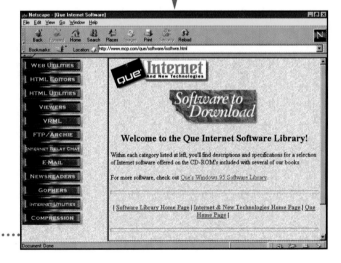

5 *Download files.* Whether you're looking for software utilities or pictures of cats, it's easy to download the files you want directly to your personal system. See Part 11 for more information on downloading files.

6 *Chat with other Internet users.* Participate in real-time "chat" sessions with Internet users from around the world—using your computer keyboard and monitor. See Part 12 for more information on Internet chat. ■

What You Need to Connect to the Internet

You connect to the Internet via your normal telephone line, to which you connect a modem, which is in turn connected to your personal computer. Once your PC is connected to the Internet (via the modem and phone line), you can use your computer to perform all your Internet-related tasks.

Can you connect your current PC to the Internet? Probably. Note, however, that to get the most from the World Wide Web (which uses a lot of graphics, sound, and video), you may need a newer, more powerful computer model. If all you're doing is checking an occasional piece of e-mail (i.e., you're *not* Web surfing!), you can get by with a lot less. It's only when you start to cruise the Web that you need to beef up your system.

So what kind of computer system do you really need to connect to the Internet? While just about any PC with a modem will do, here's what I recommend to get the most from today's Web-centric Internet:

- A Pentium-based PC, with at least 16M of memory and at least 200M free hard disk space. (You'll need the memory and disk space to handle graphic-intensive Web pages.)

- A color monitor running at least 800×600 resolution. (The extra resolution—beyond standard VGA quality—is necessary to see the entire width of some big Web pages.)

- A sound card with external speakers (to hear all the neat multimedia sound files on cutting-edge Web sites).

- A modem capable of at least 28,800bps. (Anything less makes the Web seem pretty slow.)

- Either the Windows 95 or Windows NT operating system. (The best new Internet-related software is written for these 32-bit Windows systems—*not* for the older Windows 3.X operating system.)

- A standard telephone line (although a second line dedicated to your PC might be handy if you do a *lot* of Web cruising and don't want to tie up your normal phone line).

- An account with an Internet service provider (you'll use your modem to dial your ISP and connect to the Internet)

- Appropriate Internet software, which typically includes a Web browser (such as Netscape Communicator or Internet Explorer) and perhaps dedicated e-mail and newsreader programs. (Note, however, that both Communicator and Explorer include e-mail and newsreader components, so all you really need is one of these two programs.)

Faster Connections: ISDN and Beyond

Today's typical Internet connection uses normal phone lines and modems that communicate at approximately 28,800 bits per second (bps). But there are other ways to connect to the Net that, while not yet widespread, are much faster.

One of these methods uses a phone company protocol called ISDN. *ISDN* lines (which can cost as little as $50/month, depending on your local phone company) typically transmit data at four times the rate of a standard modem. Other connection methods are a bit more futuristic. But, given the speed at which all Internet-related things change, look for devices such as cable modems and direct satellite feeds to become popular by the end of the century.

WebTV: The Internet Without a Computer

Until recently, you needed a computer to connect to the Internet. However, that's all changed with the introduction of devices that hook up to your television set (and your phone lines) and hook your TV to the Internet—no computer required. The most popular of these devices is called WebTV, and it hooks up to your television just like a VCR does; in fact, the WebTV box looks a little like a VCR, complete with a remote control so you can surf the Net from the comfort of your couch.

The WebTV box functions kind of like a dedicated computer for Internet-only tasks and uses your television set as the computer "monitor." A modem is built right into the WebTV box, so all you have to do is hook one cable from the WebTV box to your phone line and another from the box to your TV set. Then you're ready to surf the Internet—no computer necessary!

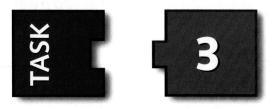

TASK **3**

How to Find an Internet Service Provider

Before you can connect to the Internet, you need to establish an account with a firm that provides Internet service—an *Internet service provider*. There are thousands of ISPs in the U.S. alone, many of which are locally based. In addition, there are several large national ISPs, most of which provide local numbers for you to dial into (so you don't rack up long-distance phone bills).

You can also connect to the Internet via one of the major commercial online services, such as America Online or the Microsoft Network. These services provide Internet access in addition to their normal proprietary content; a standard ISP, on the other hand, offers no content, just access.

Should You Use an ISP or a Commercial Online Service?

Generally, ISPs offer better connections (faster speed and better access) than busy services like America Online, and their prices are often slightly cheaper. However, it's often easier to navigate the Net via a commercial service because you get to use the same sophisticated interfaces they provide for the rest of their services. In addition, you get all the extra content that an America Online or a CompuServe Interactive provides. In reality, you can't go too wrong either way.

What Do You Need to Establish an Account with an ISP?

When you call an ISP to set up an account, all you need is your phone number and credit card (so the ISP can set up their monthly billing and bill you directly to your credit card). You may also be asked about what kind of PC system you have, particularly the speed of your modem. (Some ISPs have different dial-up numbers for different modem speeds.)

How Much Will You Pay for Internet Access?

At the time I was writing this book, most ISPs were offering some sort of unlimited monthly access for around $20 a month. Be wary of any ISP who charges an hourly fee; if you do a lot of Net cruising, you can run up some pretty hefty bills!

What Do You Get When You Establish an Account with an ISP?

In addition to your user name, password, and e-mail address, many ISPs will also send you (via disk or CD-ROM) a packet of Internet software and utilities to get you started on the Net; these typically include a browser, a separate e-mail client, and perhaps a newsgroup reader. If you're signing up with a commercial online service (such as America Online), you'll receive a CD-ROM with the software to access their proprietary service and content.

Missing Link

If you're dealing with an ISP (*not* a commercial service!), you don't have to use the software they provide. After you connect to the Internet, you're free to download whatever software you want. Plus, you can always use any commercial programs you can find at your local computer store. (If you're connecting to the Internet via America Online or another commercial service, you're tied to using their software. Sorry.)

What Makes for a Good Internet Service Provider?

There are three major things to look for in an ISP:

- **Price.** You don't have to overpay; there is enough competition among ISPs to enable you to get the lowest price possible without a lot of haggling.

- **Reliable local dial-up connection.** Make sure the ISP isn't so popular that you never get a free dial tone, and make sure that the ISP can deliver the fastest speed your modem is capable of.

- **Technical support.** If you have trouble with your account, you want to get it fixed when you're home using it. So look for an ISP with extra-long tech support hours.

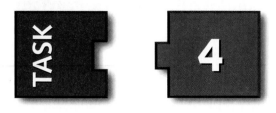

TASK 4

How to Make the Internet Safe for Kids

An almost limitless amount of information is available to you on the Internet; unfortunately, not all of it is appropriate for users of all ages. Although you want your kids to be able to use the Internet for fun and education, you will probably want to protect them from whatever harmful content they might stumble across.

The best way to make the Internet safe for your children is to surf the Net with them. There is simply no substitution for parental involvement when it comes to protecting your children.

But if you can't always be by their sides when they're surfing, you can turn to one of the numerous "kid-safe" software programs that filter out offensive content on the Net. These programs work in conjunction with your normal Internet access software by compiling lists of offensive sites (or, in some cases, offensive words) and automatically blocking access to those sites. When unauthorized users try to access a filtered site, they receive a message informing them that the site is blocked.

Such programs let you establish multiple users for your Internet account; each user has his/her own password. This way, parents can still access adult-oriented sites (with their own passwords), while children are denied access.

All of these programs look for offensive content in various categories, including sex, language, adult situations, violence, and drugs. The following table lists the most popular filtering software.

Publishers of Filtering Software

Software	Web Site	Phone Number
Cyber Patrol	http://www.cyberpatrol.com	800-828-2608
CYBERsitter	http://www.solidoak.com/index.html	800-388-2761
Net Nanny	http://www.netnanny.com	800-340-7177
SurfWatch	http://www.surfwatch.com	888-6SPYGLASS

If you're using Microsoft's Internet Explorer as your Web browser, you can take advantage of its built-in filtering capabilities. Just pull down the **View** menu, select **Options**, and click the **Security** tab. In the section labeled Content Advisor, you can click the **Settings** button to set acceptable levels for different types of content (language, nudity, sex, and violence). When you finish, click the **Enable Ratings** button to turn on the built-in filter.

Another solution is to use a Web site specifically designed as a kid-safe "front end" to the Internet. One such site is Bess (located at **http://www.bess.com**). You simply set Bess as the default starter page for your Web browser, and the site itself limits access to unacceptable Web sites.

Note that these are all solutions to a sticky dilemma facing the online community. How do you protect sensitive users (particularly children) from the bad things on the Internet, while at the same time avoiding censorship of controversial content? Do you want access to everything available online, or do you want it "pre-filtered" according to someone else's morals and tastes? When does limiting access to certain types of information become censorship?

There are some who want to dictate what can and cannot be made available over the Internet. Personally, I like the compromise solution: giving users access to everything, but providing filtering software so that each user can decide whether to block access to certain types of content for specific family members. This is the online equivalent of changing the channel on your television when you see something you don't like; it enables you to protect your family without imposing your views on others.

PART II

Three Ways to Connect to the Internet

WHILE THERE ARE HUNDREDS of companies that will offer to connect you to the Internet, Internet access comes in three basic flavors. Which flavor you pick depends on your needs.

These are the three basic types of Internet service:

- **Dedicated Internet Service Provider.** This is either a local company or a national firm with local phone numbers whose only business is connecting you (via your phone line) directly to the Internet. ISPs don't offer any bells and whistles or proprietary content, and some don't even provide you with software.

- **Commercial Online Service.** Four major worldwide services (America Online, CompuServe Interactive, The Microsoft Network, and Prodigy Internet) can provide you with proprietary content, a proprietary interface, and—as an added feature—access to all or part of the Internet. These commercial services offer you the ultimate in hand holding, at the trade off of some degree of flexibility. (Remember, the Internet is *not* their primary business!)

- **WebTV.** This service is offered to purchasers of the WebTV set-top box sold by Sony and Phillips/Magnavox. You can't get to WebTV from your computer, just as you can't get to any of the other services from your TV.

Which type of service should you choose? It depends on what you need. If you want the fastest service possible and want to choose your own Internet software, choose an ISP. If, on the other hand, you want the easiest possible connection and a familiar interface, choose one of the commercial online services, such as America Online. And, of course, if you're connecting via a WebTV box, you have only one choice: WebTV.

(Personally, I connect all three ways. I use my ISP for my hard-core Internet access, where speed is of the essence. I also have accounts with all four commercial services, primarily for their proprietary content—although I do use CompuServe for my Internet access when I'm on the road because they have local access numbers in all major U.S. cities. And, finally, I use WebTV to do some quick browsing during the evening when I'm parked in front of my television set. As you can see, each kind of access has its advantages!)

Where can you find an Internet service provider? There are several places to look, the first of which is probably your local Yellow Pages phone directory, under the "Internet" heading. To make your search a little easier, I've listed some of the more popular national ISPs and commercial services in the table below.

In addition, c|net (a major provider of computer-related information on the Internet) has prepared a comparison of the most popular local and national ISPs. If you already have access to the Web, you can find this comparison at the following address: **http://www.cnet. com/Content/Reviews/Compare/ISP**. (If you just want a big list of ISPs—currently at 4,445

entries and counting—check out "The List" from iWORLD at **http://thelist.iworld.com**.)

Read the tasks in this section to learn more about the three gateways to the Internet.

Missing Link

The Internet is an ever-changing medium. Web sites are constantly revising their content, and Web browsers are constantly being updated to keep pace with advances in content. Although the screens shown in this book are of the most recent versions of Web pages and software at the time of printing, what you see on the Internet might be different.

Major Internet Service Providers

Service	Web Site	Phone Number
America Online	http://www.aol.com	800-827-6364
AT&T WorldNet	http://www.att.com/worldnet/wis	800-967-5363
CompuServe Interactive	http://www.compuserve.com	800-524-3388
GTE Internet Solutions	http://www.gte.net	800-363-8483
MCI Internet Dial Access	http://www.mci.com	800-550-0927
The Microsoft Network	http://www.msn.com	800-386-5550
Netcom	http://www.netcom.com	800-353-6600
Prodigy Internet	http://www.prodigy.com	800-776-3449
Sprint Internet Passport	http://www.sprint.com/sip	800-359-3900
WebTV	http://www.webtv.net	800-GOWEBTV

Connecting Through an Internet Service Provider

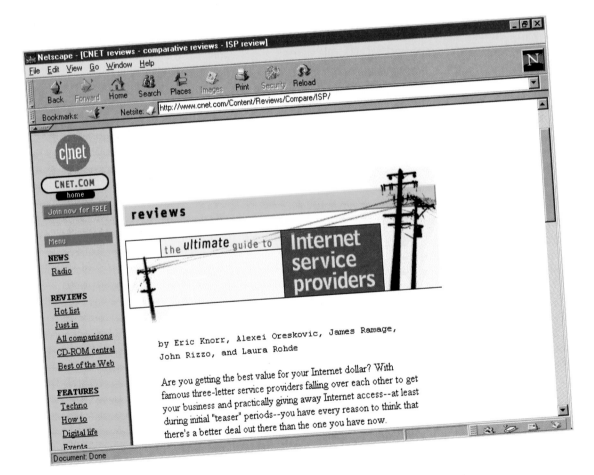

The most popular way to connect to the Internet is through a dedicated Internet service provider (ISP). ISPs provide you with a gateway to the Internet; you use your computer and modem to dial into the ISP, which then connects you directly to the Internet.

There are literally thousands of ISPs in the U.S. alone. Some are big national companies or organizations; others are small local companies or organizations. They all do essentially the same thing: connect you to the Internet. If you have access to the Web, I recommend you check out the list of ISPs (along with ratings) prepared by c|net, a popular computer-oriented site on the Web. You can find c|net's list at the following address:

http://www.cnet.com/Content/ Reviews/Compare/ISP

Which kind of ISP should you use: a local ISP or a big national ISP? There are pluses and minuses to using each kind of provider.

Local providers have the advantage of being local—with local offices and local phone numbers. Most local ISPs are relatively small businesses, with all the pros and cons of a small business. Local ISPs can be financially unstable, might not offer enough lines to handle a large number of subscribers, and might not have the most professional (or most available, time-of-day-wise) technical support. On the other hand, local ISPs often have faster dial-in connections sooner than the national ISPs do, because they have fewer lines to upgrade.

Business-wise, national ISPs are definitely more stable than local ISPs. You'll find that they offer very professional installation software and technical support, and often lower monthly rates. On the other hand, some national ISPs are slow to upgrade their technology (sticking you with slower connect speeds). In addition, they might be impersonal to deal with and might not even have a local number for you to use.

After you decide which is best for you, follow these steps to establish a connection with an Internet service provider:

1. Contact the ISP to which you want to subscribe. The ISP will send you an installation kit, either on disk or CD-ROM.

2. Install the software on your PC. If an ISP doesn't provide you with software, you should get a set of instructions on how to configure your Windows 95 Dial-Up Networking feature for access to the ISP's Internet gateway.

3. Dial into the ISP to establish your account. (Follow the instructions given to you by your ISP.) When your account is established, your ISP will assign you a member ID, a password, and an e-mail address.

Missing Link

In many cases, you'll be connecting to an ISP via Windows 95's Dial-Up Networking function. Many ISPs let you use Windows 95's Internet Connection Wizard to help automate your Dial-Up Networking Internet setup.

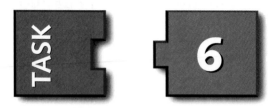

TASK **6**

Connecting Through a Commercial Online Service

To many people, using an ISP to connect to the Internet is a little daunting. There is a solution, however: commercial online services. A commercial online service provides its paying subscribers with a wealth of proprietary content (that which is not available anyplace else,

including on the Web). It uses a custom interface for easy navigation, and it provides a lot of added-value features and hand holding. In addition, all the online services now offer access to most, if not all, of the Internet—which makes America Online and the like the *easiest* way to get on the Net for a lot of people.

There are four major commercial online services:

- **America Online.** AOL is the largest online service in the world, with more than 8 million subscribers in the U.S. alone. Because of its size, it also is able to obtain the most proprietary content—content that you won't find on the Web. AOL's Internet service is okay, but it's not the fastest in the world. (You can find AOL on the Web at **http://www.aol.com**.)

- **CompuServe Interactive.** CompuServe is the oldest online service, but it's no longer the biggest. It has the most members outside the U.S., however, and attracts a very "professional" audience, in all types of areas. I think CompuServe does the best job of integrating its own proprietary content with access to Web content; its interface perfectly blends internal CompuServe with external Web browsing. (You can find CompuServe on the Web at **http://www.compuserve.com**.)

- **The Microsoft Network.** Launched by Microsoft coincident with the launch of Windows 95, MSN is the new kid on the block. Its interface is a customized version of Internet Explorer, and it offers the most technical bells and whistles of all the online services. The glitz comes at a price, however; MSN is horrendously slow, even on a fast connection. (You can find MSN on the Web at **http://www.msn.com**.)

- **Prodigy Internet.** Prodigy Internet is a new version of an old service. Prodigy "classic" used a proprietary, clunky-looking interface; Prodigy Internet is totally Web-based, using Internet Explorer as its software. In fact, Prodigy Internet—although it has quite a bit of proprietary content—looks a lot like a regular old Internet service provider. (You can find Prodigy on the Web at **http://www.prodigy.com**.)

Which is the best commercial service for you? The table below might help you decide. When you're ready to subscribe to the online service of your choice, follow these steps:

1. Call the 800 number of the service of your choice (they're listed in the introduction to this part). The service will send you a membership kit, which generally contains an instruction booklet and a CD-ROM.

2. Install the software on your computer, start the automatic registration program, and follow the instructions on-screen. (Make sure your credit card number is handy, of course!)

Within minutes, you'll have the software installed on your PC, you'll be assigned a membership ID and password, and your billing will be set up. It's no harder than that.

Finding the Right Online Service

Your Needs	The Right Service
You want the most proprietary content.	America Online
You want the best integration of Web and proprietary content.	CompuServe Interactive
You don't care about content; you really want an ISP.	Prodigy Internet
You want lots of glitz and an ultra-fast connection.	The Microsoft Network

TASK 7

Connecting Through WebTV

WebTV is the Internet without a computer—kind of like the Internet for regular folks.

Actually, WebTV is both a type of electronics device and a specific Internet gateway. The electronics device (sold under both the Sony and Phillips/Magnavox brands) looks a little like a small VCR: It's a box small enough to sit on top of your television set. At around $300, it's more affordable than a complete personal computer system, yet it will serve the purpose if all you want to do is surf the Net.

When you unpack your WebTV box, the first thing you do is connect it to a power outlet, to your television set (using standard audio/video cables), and to your telephone line. The first time you turn on the WebTV box, it uses an 800-number to dial into a national database and find a local phone number. From that point on, it uses the local number to connect you to WebTV headquarters, where you sign up for the WebTV Internet service. (As you do for other signup procedures, have your credit card number handy.)

The WebTV service (which currently runs approximately $20/month for unlimited access) is a special "front end" to the Internet. The WebTV screens are specifically designed for optimal viewing on a normal television set. It's a very user-friendly interface and makes the Internet a lot easier to use than what some PC users are accustomed to.

At this point in time, WebTV offers access to only the World Wide Web and e-mail. If you want to access UseNet newsgroups or download files, you should use a traditional PC-based Internet service. The folks at WebTV promise more services in the future, many of which can be automatically downloaded from the Internet direct to your WebTV box.

You operate your WebTV box with a wireless remote control that's similar to the one you use for your television set. The difference is that the WebTV remote has some dedicated buttons just for WebTV operations, including both directional arrows and two "scroll" buttons (for scrolling through long Web pages).

You can also operate WebTV with an optional wireless keyboard. I recommend spending the extra $70 or so for this device; not only does it make entering information into search boxes a lot easier, it also has more dedicated keys for specific WebTV functions (such as saving a favorite page or going directly to a specific Web page).

If you don't buy the keyboard, you have to use the regular remote control (with no alphabetical keys) to enter search terms and other information. If you use the remote for this purpose, WebTV displays a pop-up virtual keyboard on screen; you then use the directional keys on the remote to "hunt and peck" the letters and numbers you want.

To recap, here's how you access the Internet via WebTV:

1. Go to your local consumer electronics store and buy either a Sony or a Phillips/Magnavox WebTV box (hopefully with the optional wireless keyboard).

2. Connect the WebTV box to your TV and your phone line.

3. Turn on the WebTV box and follow the on-screen instructions to register for the WebTV service.

Missing Link

You can get more information about WebTV at the following Web site:

http://www.webtv.net

PART III

Six Ways to Surf the Internet

8 Surfing with Netscape Communicator

9 Surfing with Internet Explorer

10 Surfing with America Online

11 Surfing with The Microsoft Network

12 Surfing with CompuServe Interactive

13 Surfing with WebTV

IN PART 2, YOU LEARNED how to obtain Internet connection service. Now that you're connected to the Net, it's time to choose the software you'll use to surf the Web, read and write e-mail messages, and communicate with UseNet newsgroups.

There are lots of choices available, but the method you select will partially depend on the type of Internet access you selected. While there are literally dozens of options, I've selected the six most popular ones to outline in this part:

- Using **Netscape Communicator** as your "suite" of software programs. (This requires a connection through an Internet service provider, as described in Task 5.) The Web browser in Communicator is called Navigator; Communicator also includes e-mail, newsreader, and Web page composer programs. You can obtain a "trial" copy of Communicator at Netscape's Web site (**http://www.netscape.com**), or you can purchase a boxed version at retail. Actually, many ISPs provide you with Netscape's software free-of-charge when you open an Internet service account, so you may not have to get it on your own at all.

- Using Microsoft's **Internet Explorer** and its e-mail and newsreader components as your main Internet software. (This requires a connection through an Internet service provider, as described in Task 5.) You can obtain a free version of Explorer at Microsoft's Web site (located at **http://www.microsoft.com**), or you can purchase an "added-value" boxed version at retail. Again, many ISPs provide you with Microsoft's software free-of-charge when you open an Internet service account, so you might not have to get it on your own.

- Using **America Online** as your "front end" to the Internet. (This requires AOL membership, as described in Task 6.) America Online uses its own proprietary software for its Internet connection; AOL will ship you their software when you open a new account.

- Using **The Microsoft Network** as your "front end" to the Internet. (This requires MSN membership, as described in Task 6.) MSN uses its own proprietary software—which is based on Internet Explorer—for its Internet connection; MSN will ship you their software when you open a new account.

- Using **CompuServe Interactive** as your "front end" to the Internet. (This requires CompuServe membership, as described in Task 6.) CompuServe uses its own proprietary software for its Internet connection; CompuServe will ship you their software when you open a new account.

- Using **WebTV** to connect to the Internet. (This requires the purchase of a WebTV box, as well as a subscription to WebTV's Internet service, as described in Task 7.) The WebTV software is built into the WebTV box; you do not have to purchase or install anything else.

Which of these programs should you use? Well, depending on your connection, the choice might be made for you. If you're using WebTV, you have no choice; WebTV, it is. Same thing with MSN. However, both AOL and CompuServe have options that let you use an external Web browser, such as Internet Explorer or Netscape Navigator, instead of their proprietary interfaces.

If you're using an ISP, you have a real choice for your Web browser: Netscape Navigator (in the Communicator suite) or Microsoft's Internet Explorer. They both perform in pretty much the same manner and have pretty much the same features. As I write this book, Navigator is far and away the most popular of the two; Internet Explorer is coming up strong, however. You won't go wrong using either of these two programs.

Because all of these programs offer similar capabilities—but with their own unique methods of operation—use the following tasks as a type of "quick reference" to the featured Internet gateway.

For more detailed information about each of these programs/services, check out Que's library of helpful books at your local bookseller or online at **http://www.mcp.com/que/**.

Surfing with Netscape Communicator

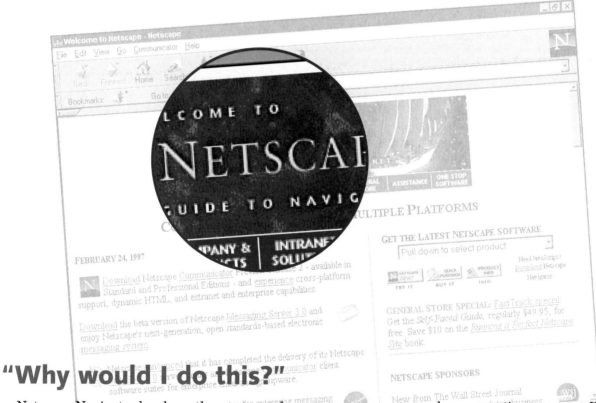

"Why would I do this?"

Netscape Navigator has been the most popular Web browser for the past several years. Now, in addition to version 4.0 of Navigator, Netscape has created a complete suite of software programs (called Netscape Communicator) for all aspects of Internet access. Netscape Communicator includes components for e-mail, newsgroups, and even creating your own Web pages. This section shows you the basics of Communicator operation. (This task was written on a "preview" release of Communicator; some of the screens may look different in the final released version.)

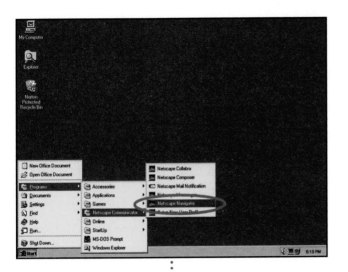

1 The Netscape Communicator suite comprises several components. The Web browser is called Netscape Navigator. You can access it and all other Communicator programs from this main program. To launch Navigator, double-click its icon on the Windows 95 Start menu.

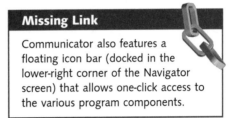

Missing Link

Communicator also features a floating icon bar (docked in the lower-right corner of the Navigator screen) that allows one-click access to the various program components.

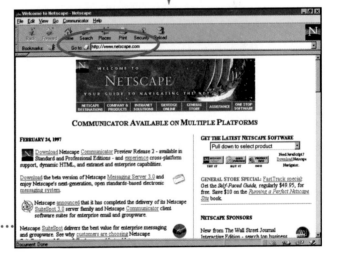

2 To go to a specific site on the Web, enter the site's Web address (URL) in the **Go to:** text box and press **Enter**.

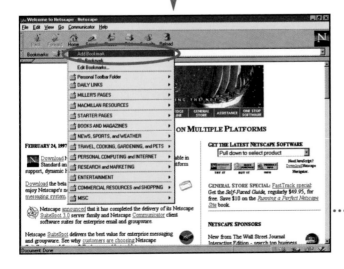

3 Click the **Bookmarks** button to see a list of your favorite sites. To add a site to the bookmark list, click the **Bookmarks** button and select **Add Bookmarks**.

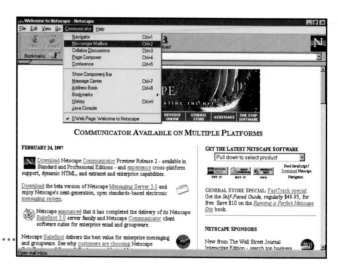

4 To access Communicator's e-mail program, pull down Navigator's **Communicator** menu and select **Messenger Mailbox**.

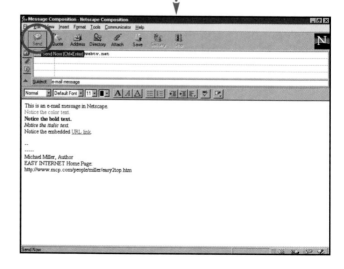

5 When the Inbox window appears, click the **Get Msg** button to check for your latest messages. Select the message you want to read in the top pane; the message itself is displayed in the bottom pane. Click the **Reply** button to reply to the current message.

6 To create a new e-mail message, click the Inbox's **New Msg** button. When the Composition window appears, fill in the **To:** and **Subject:** fields, and then enter the text of your message in the large text box. Click the **Send** button to send your completed message.

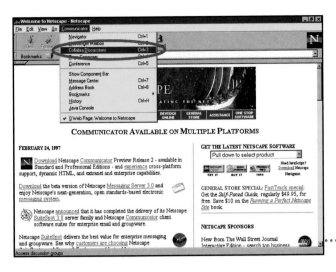

7 To access Communicator's newsreader component, pull down Navigator's **Communicator** menu and select **Collabra Discussions**.

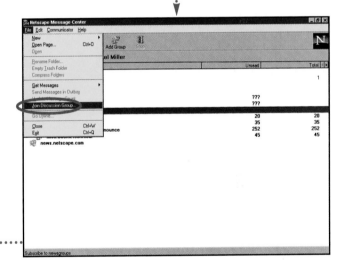

8 To see a complete list of UseNet newsgroups, pull down the **File** menu and select **Join Discussion Group**.

9 When the Subscribe to a Discussion Group dialog box appears, select one or more newsgroups, click the **Subscribe** button, and then click **OK**.

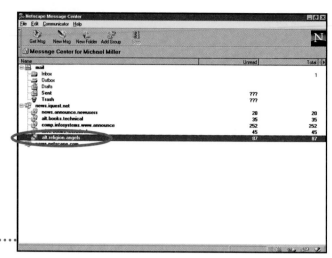

10 To view all the messages in a subscribed newsgroup, double-click the newsgroup in the Message Center window.

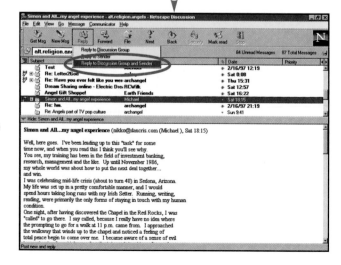

11 Newsgroup message headers now appear in the top pane. Click the message you want to read, and the contents of the selected message appear in the bottom pane.

12 To reply to the current message, click the **Reply** button and select **Reply to Discussion Group and Sender**. (This posts your reply to the entire newsgroup and sends an e-mail message to the person who posted the original message.) Click **Send** when you're ready to post your reply. ■

Surfing with Internet Explorer

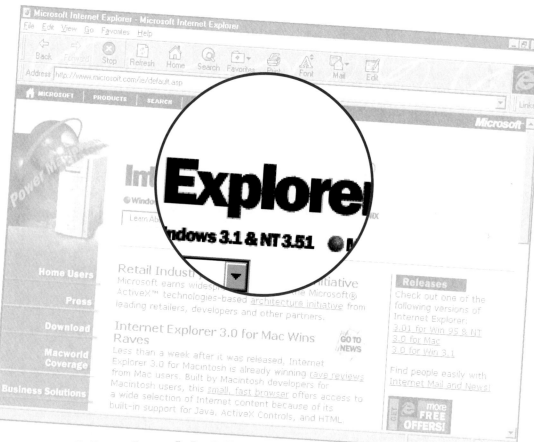

"Why would I do this?"

Microsoft's Internet Explorer is the "up and coming" Web browser, a strong competitor for Netscape Navigator. Internet Explorer is more than just a Web browser, however; it also includes components for e-mail and news-groups. This section shows you the basics of Internet Explorer operation.

1 To go to a specific site on the Web, enter the site's Web address (URL) in the **Address** box, and then press **Enter**.

2 Click the **Stop** button to stop the current Web page from loading; click the **Refresh** button to reload the current page.

3 Click the **Favorites** button to access your list of favorites. You can choose a page from the list to go directly to it. To add a page to your Favorites list, click the **Favorites** button and select **Add to Favorites**.

4 To read waiting e-mail, click Internet Explorer's **Mail** button and select **Read Mail**.

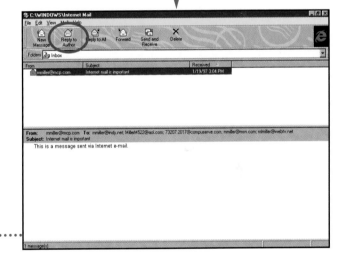

5 When the Inbox window appears, click the **Send and Receive** button to check for your latest messages. Select the message you want to read from the top pane, and the text of that message appears in the bottom pane. Click the **Reply to Author** button to reply to this message.

6 To create a new e-mail message, click the **New Message** button. Fill in the **To:** and **Subject:** fields, and then enter the text of your message in the large text box. Click the **Send** button to send your completed message.

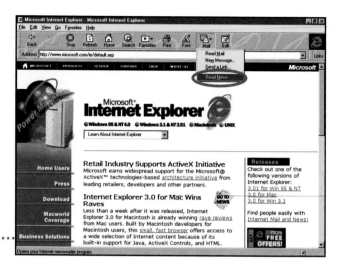

7 To access UseNet newsgroups, click Internet Explorer's **Mail** button and select **Read News**.

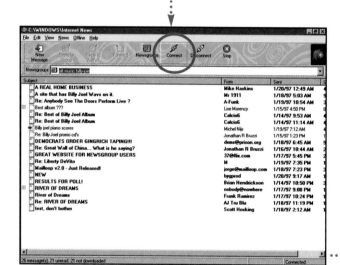

8 When the newsreader window appears, click the **Connect** button to connect to your news server.

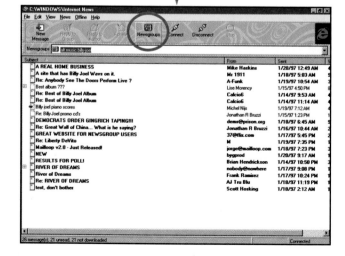

9 To see a complete list of newsgroups, click the **Newsgroups** button.

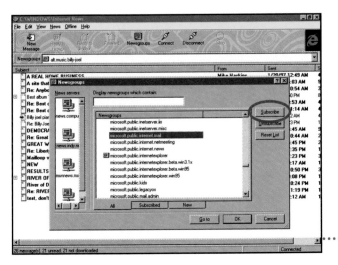

10 Select one or more groups from the list, click the **Subscribe** button, and then click **OK**.

11 When the list of articles in the selected newsgroup appears, double-click the article you want to read.

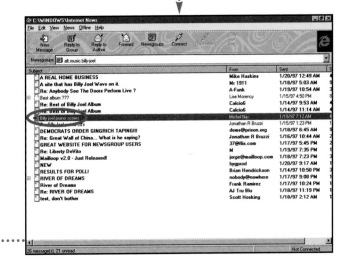

12 When the message window appears, click the **Reply to Group** button to reply to this message. Click the **Post Message** button when you're ready to post your reply. ■

Surfing with America Online

"Why would I do this?"

More than eight million people access the Internet via America Online, the world's most popular commercial online service. AOL includes a variety of Internet features, including a built-in Web browser, e-mail, and newsgroup access. This section shows you the basics of America Online's Internet operations.

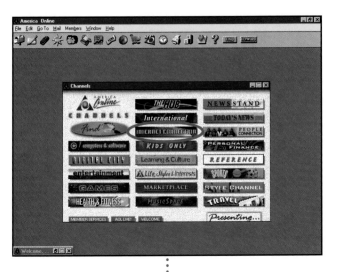

1 To access America Online's Internet features, click **Internet Connection**.

Puzzled?

If you get a busy signal when trying to connect to AOL, don't fret. AOL, like many other online services, sometimes gets too busy for its own good; it can handle only so many members at a time. Try calling back in a few minutes or at a less popular time of the day.

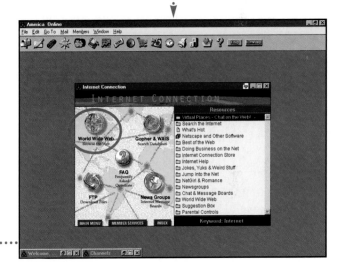

2 To access AOL's Web browser, click **World Wide Web**.

3 To go to a specific site on the Web, enter the site's Web address (URL) in the **Address** box, and then press **Enter**.

4 When AOL's home page appears, you have the option of immediately beginning an Internet search. To begin a search, enter your search terms in the box and click **Search**.

5 To save the current page as one of your Favorite Places, click the "heart" icon.

6 To view a list of your Favorite Places, click the **Favorite Places** icon on AOL's toolbar.

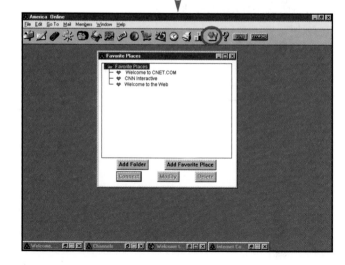

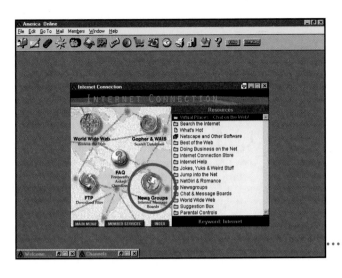

7 To access UseNet newsgroups, click **News Groups** on AOL's Internet screen.

8 To subscribe to newsgroups, click the **Add Newsgroups** icon to see a list of what's available. Then select the group(s) to which you want to subscribe.

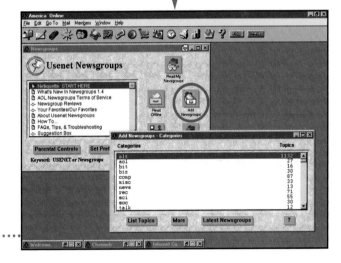

9 To view articles in your subscribed groups, click the **Read My Newsgroups** icon, select a group from the list, select the message you want to read, and then click **Read**.

10 To read e-mail messages, click the **Read New Mail** icon (the mailbox) on AOL's toolbar.

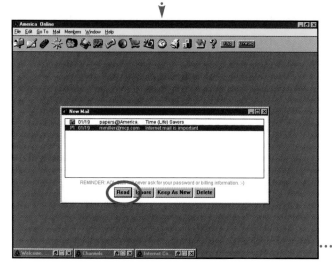

11 In the New Mail dialog box, select the desired message and click **Read**.

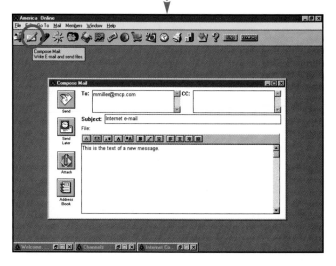

12 To create a new e-mail message, click the **Compose Mail** icon on AOL's toolbar. Fill in the **To:** and **Subject:** fields, and then enter the text of your message in the large text box. Click **Send** to send your completed message. ■

Surfing with The Microsoft Network

"Why would I do this?"

The Microsoft Network is the latest competitor in the commercial online services field. Because it's run by Microsoft, you can find an MSN icon on the desktop of just about every computer running the Windows 95 operating system. Not surprisingly, MSN's software is actually a customized version of Internet Explorer; it even uses the same e-mail and newsgroup programs that Explorer does. This section shows you the basics of MSN's Internet operations.

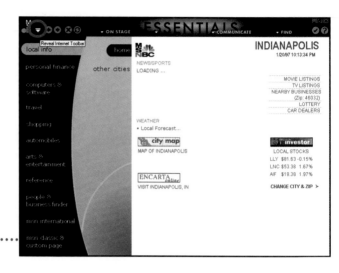

1 Click the down arrow to reveal MSN's Internet toolbar.

2 To go to a specific site on the Web, enter the site's Web address (URL) in the **Address** box, and then click **Enter**.

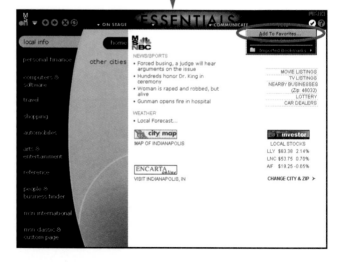

3 To add the current page to your Favorites list, click the "check mark" icon and select **Add To Favorites**. (You also click this icon to display and choose from the pages on your Favorites list.)

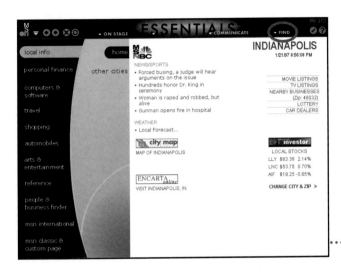

4 To search the Internet, click **Find**.

5 Click the **Word** tab to search for words or phrases.

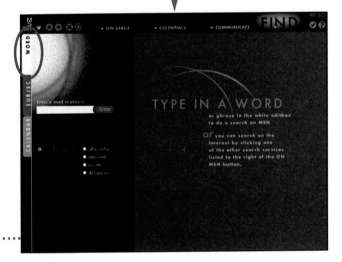

6 Enter your search term in the blank, select your preferred search engine (**MSN**, **AltaVista**, **Excite**, **InfoSeek**, or **DejaNews**), and then click **Enter**.

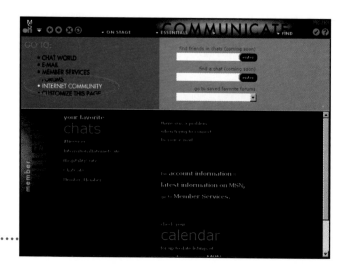

7 To access UseNet newsgroups, click **Communicate** (located at the top of the MSN screen), and then click **Internet Community**.

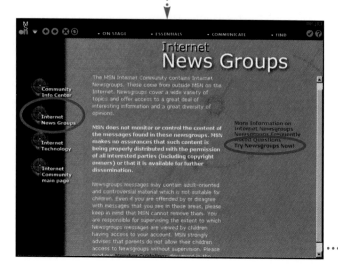

8 When the next screen appears, click **Internet News Groups**. Read the text if you want to, and click **Try Newsgroups Now!** when you're ready to get going again.

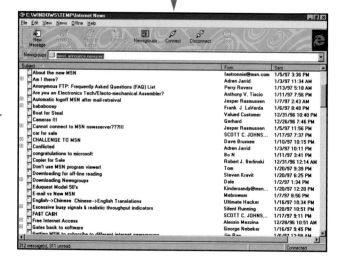

9 MSN launches Microsoft's newsreader software. You can refer to Task 9 for instructions on how to view messages.

10 To read and write e-mail messages, return to the MSN opening screen, click **Communicate**, and then click **E-Mail**. MSN launches Microsoft's e-mail software.

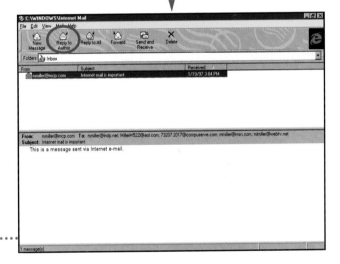

11 To read a waiting message, select the message in the top pane, and its contents appear in the bottom pane. You can click the **Reply to Author** button to reply to the selected message.

12 To create a new e-mail message, click the **New Message** button. Fill in the **To:** and **Subject:** fields, and then enter the text of your message in the large text box. Click the **Send** button to send your completed message. ■

Surfing with CompuServe Interactive

"Why would I do this?"

CompuServe is the oldest online service, and it offers perhaps the best integration of Web access and proprietary content. Like MSN, CompuServe uses a version of Internet Explorer

as its Web browser; however, it's so well integrated into CompuServe's main interface that you'll hardly know where CompuServe ends and the Web starts. This section shows you the basics of CompuServe's Internet operations.

1 To access CompuServe's Internet features, go to the main menu and click **Internet**.

2 To search the Internet, click **Search**. When the search page appears, enter your search phrase in the text box and click **Find It**.

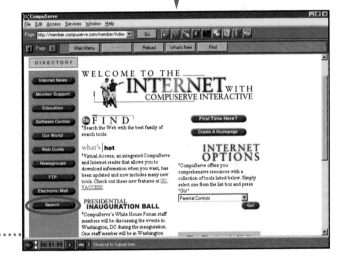

3 To go to a specific site on the Web, enter the site's Web address (URL) in the **Page** box, and then press **Enter**. The Web page will be displayed on your CompuServe screen.

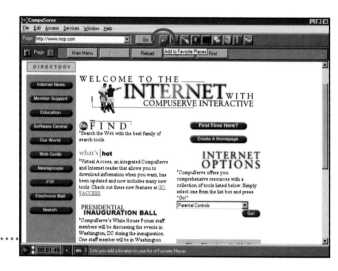

4 To add the current page to your Favorite Places list, click the **Add to Favorite Places** icon on CompuServe's toolbar.

5 To view your Favorite Places list, click the **Favorite Places** icon on CompuServe's toolbar. When the Favorite Places dialog box appears, select the site you want to go to, and then click **Go**.

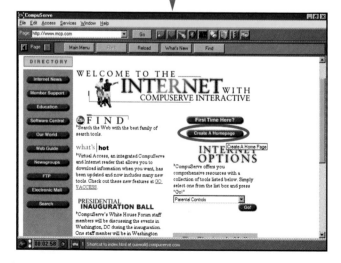

6 To create your own home page (as part of CompuServe's Our World personal home page site), click **Create a Homepage**.

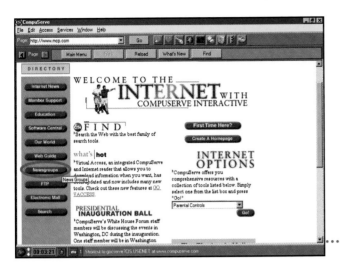

7 To access UseNet newsgroups, click **Newsgroups**. When the next dialog box appears, select **USENET Newsreader (CIM)**.

8 To view a list of newsgroups, select **Subscribe to Newsgroups**. If you want to subscribe to any newsgroups, select one or more groups from the list and click **Subscribe**.

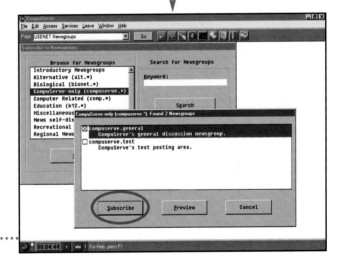

9 To read newsgroup articles, select **Access Your USENET Newsgroups**, select the group, select an article, and then click **Get**.

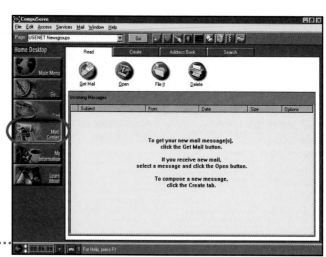

10 To read and write e-mail messages, go to CompuServe's main menu and click the **Mail Center** button.

11 To read e-mail messages, select the **Read** tab and click **Get Mail**. Select the message you want to read, and then click **Open**.

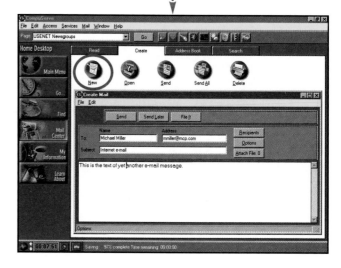

12 To create new e-mail messages, select the **Create** tab and click **New**. Fill in the **To:** and **Subject:** fields, and then enter the text of your message in the large text box. Click **Send** to send your completed message. ■

Surfing with WebTV

"Why would I do this?"

The newest way to access the Internet doesn't use a personal computer—it uses your television set! First, you must buy a WebTV box (from Sony or Phillips/Magnavox), which contains everything you need to access the Internet— except for a display device, which is where your TV comes in. WebTV offers an attractive, non-threatening way to access the Internet, even if it limits its features to e-mail and the Web (no newsgroups). This section shows you the basics of WebTV's operations.

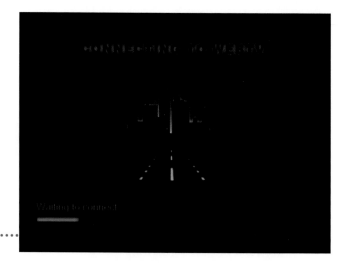

1 When you power up the WebTV unit, you're shown a screen that displays the connection progress.

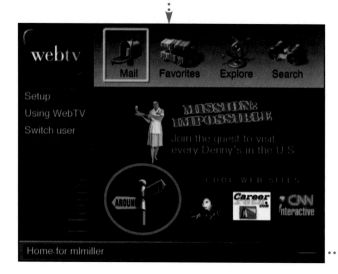

2 Once the connection is made, the WebTV home page appears automatically. Click any icon—such as the **Around Town** icon—to visit the highlighted site.

3 To go to a specific Web page, press the **Options** button on the remote control to display the Options menu. Click **Go To**. (If you are using the remote, click **Go** to bring up the on-screen keyboard.) Then fill in the address of the page you want to visit and click **Go to Page**.

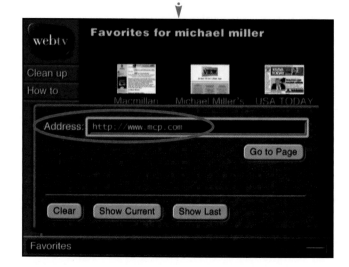

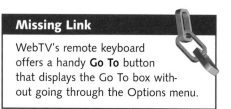

Missing Link

WebTV's remote keyboard offers a handy **Go To** button that displays the Go To box without going through the Options menu.

4 To browse through a collection of your favorite Web pages, click the **Favorites** icon on the WebTV home page or the **Favorites** button on the remote.

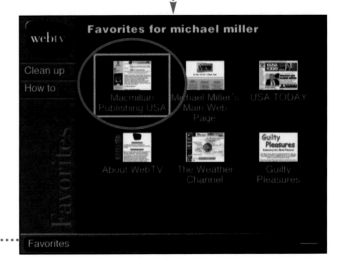

5 This page contains a collection of your favorite pages, displaying a "thumbnail" of each page, as well as the name of the page itself. Click the "thumbnail" for a favorite page to go directly to that page.

6 To add a page to your favorites collection, begin by going to that page. Then press the **Options** button on the remote control to display the Options menu, and click **Save** to add the page to your favorites collection.

Missing Link

If you're using the wireless keyboard, you can bypass the Options menu by pressing the **Save** button. (The normal remote control doesn't have a Save button.)

7 To explore a variety of topics, click the **Explore** icon on the WebTV home page.

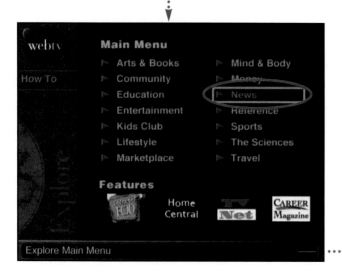

8 A list of topics appears. Click a topic to see the Web pages associated with that topic.

9 WebTV has pre-selected some of the most popular Web pages for each topic. Click a page link to go directly to the associated page.

10 To read and compose e-mail messages, click the **Mail** icon on the WebTV home page.

11 Messages you have received are automatically listed on screen; click any message to read it. To compose a new message, click **Write**.

12 Enter the recipient's address in the **To:** field, enter the subject of the message in the **Subject:** field, and enter the text of the message in the large message field. Click **Send** to send the message. ■

PART IV

Eight Things to Know About Browsing Web Pages

THE *WORLD WIDE WEB* IS JUST PART of the entire Internet. In particular, the Web (or WWW) is the part of the Internet where information is presented in a highly visual, often multimedia, format.

Information on the World Wide Web is presented in pages. A *Web page* is like a page in a book, made up of text and pictures (also called *graphics*). A Web page differs from a book page, however, in that it can include other elements, such as audio and video, and *links* to other Web pages.

It's this linking to other Web pages that makes the Web such a dynamic way to present information. A link on a Web page can point to another Web page from the same author, or to a page on another Web site. Most links are included as part of a Web page's text and are called *hypertext links*. (If a link is part of a graphic, it's called a *graphic link*.) Links are usually in a different color than the rest of the text, and are often underlined. Links are easy to use. Just position your cursor over a link and notice how the cursor changes shape from the normal arrow to a pointing hand. When the cursor is over the link, click your mouse button; your Web browser will automatically take you to the linked page.

Web pages reside at a Web *site*. A Web site is nothing more than a collection of Web pages (each in its own individual computer file) residing on a host computer. The host computer is connected full-time to the Internet so that you can access the site—and its Web pages—anytime you access the Internet. The main page at a Web site is called a *home page*, and it often serves as an "opening screen" that provides a brief overview and a sort of menu of everything you can find at that site. The address of a Web page is called a URL, which stands for Uniform Resource Locator.

Fortunately, you don't need to know what an URL is to access a Web page. All you have to do is enter the URL for a Web page directly into your browser's Location box, and then press the **Enter** key. This loads the Web page that resides at the address you entered into your main browser window.

I find that cruising the Web is like browsing through an encyclopedia. Invariably when I'm reading one article in an encyclopedia, I find a reference to a related article that interests me. When I turn to the new article, I find a reference to another article, which references another article…and, before I know it, I have all twenty-four volumes open in front of me. When you're on the Web, it's the same sort of experience. In the course of a single session, it's not unusual to discover that you've visited more than a dozen different sites—and still have lots of interesting places to go!

You cruise the Web using a piece of software called a *Web browser*. The two most popular browsers are Netscape Navigator (part of the Netscape Communicator suite of Internet products) and Microsoft's Internet Explorer, both of which work in similar fashion. I've used Navigator to illustrate the examples throughout this book.

This part of *Easy Internet, Second Edition* teaches you the basics of Web browsing. For more details about *where* to browse, see Parts 5, 6, 7, and 8.

Missing Link

Because the creators of Web sites put a lot of work into their sites, it's not unusual for your browser to take a long time to download the large text and graphics files needed to display sophisticated Web pages. So if you're going to be a frequent Web cruiser, you probably should invest in the highest-speed modem you can afford. Otherwise, prepare to spend a lot of time twiddling your thumbs as you watch Web pages *slo-o-o-owly* build on your screen!

Missing Link

The Internet is an ever-changing medium. Web sites are constantly revising their content, and Web browsers are constantly being updated to keep pace with advances in content. Although the screens shown in this book are of the most recent versions of Web pages and software at the time of printing, what you see on the Internet might be different.

Reading a Web Page

"Why would I do this?"

How do you read a Web page? Most Web pages are made up of the same common elements, shown on this sample page.

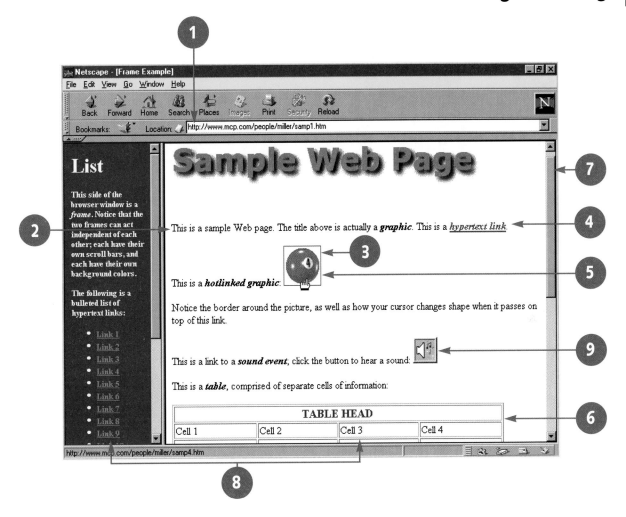

1. **URL:** The address of the current Web page.

2. **Text:** Just normal text, like you'd read in a book.

3. **Graphic:** A picture on a Web page.

4. **Hypertext link:** A text-based link to another Web page; click the underlined text to go to the linked page.

5. **Graphic link**: A graphic that, when clicked, links you to another Web page.

6. **Table**: Information presented in tabular format (like a computer spreadsheet).

7. **Scroll bars:** Bars that appear on the left and bottom edges of the window that enable you to scroll down through long Web pages.

8. **Frames**: Some Web pages are divided into parts, each of which has its own scroll bars.

9. **Sound event**: Press this button to hear a specific sound through your PC's speakers.

Navigating the Web with URLs

"Why would I do this?"

The address of a Web page is called a *Uniform Resource Locator*, or *URL*. When you enter an URL into your browser's Location box, the browser automatically takes you to the corresponding Web page.

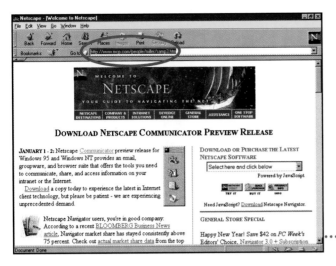

1 Enter the URL in the **Location** text box. For example, enter **http://www.mcp.com/people/miller/samp3.htm**.

2 Press the **Enter** key, and you'll be taken directly to the Web page at the address you entered. ■

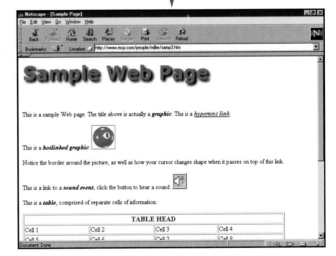

Puzzled?

If you receive an error message after entering an URL, chances are you entered it incorrectly. Remember to enter the URL *exactly* as it's written, differentiating between uppercase and lowercase letters and getting all the periods and backslashes just right. Otherwise, you could end up at a completely different Web site!

Stopping and Reloading Web Pages

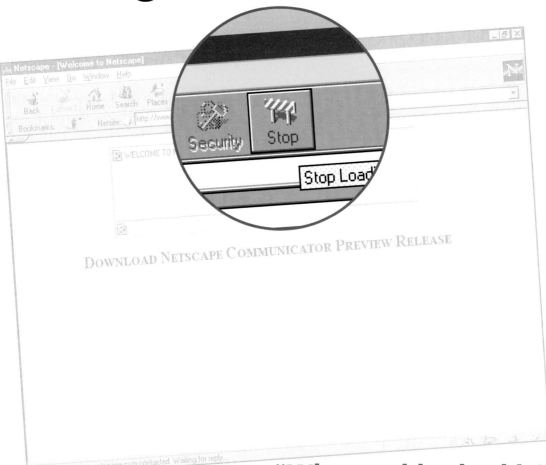

"Why would I do this?"

Sometimes Web pages take a long time to load, and sometimes they load incorrectly. When this happens, you may want to stop and start over. In addition, some pages update information at such a rapid rate that you may want to *reload* a page to get the latest information. To do this, you use the Stop and Reload buttons.

1 To stop a page from loading, click the **Stop** button before the page is finished. Either a blank page or a partial page will be displayed.

Missing Link

You can also stop a page from loading by pressing the **Esc** button on your keyboard.

2 To refresh or reload the current page, click the **Reload** button. The page will reload, starting from scratch. ■

Missing Link

If you're using Netscape Navigator, the Stop and Reload buttons are the same button. The Stop button is displayed while a page is loading; the Reload button is displayed when the page finishes loading.

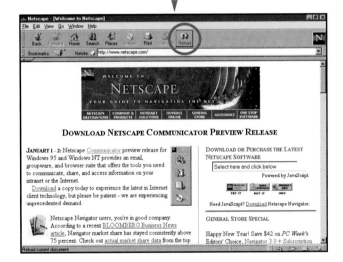

Going Home

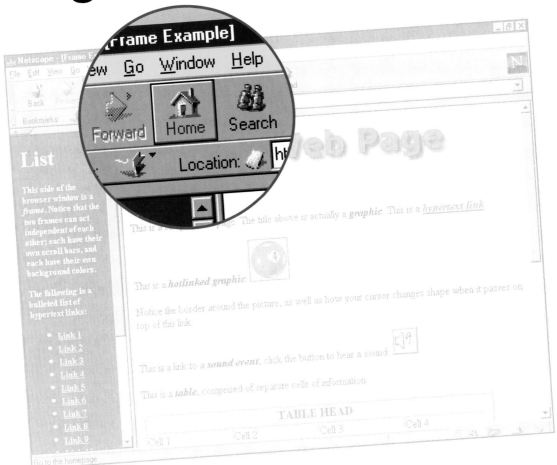

"Why would I do this?"

When you launch your browser, the very first page it displays is called the *home page* or *start page*. After you've spent a long session cruising the Web, you may want to return directly to the home page without entering the URL. To do this, you use the browser's Home button.

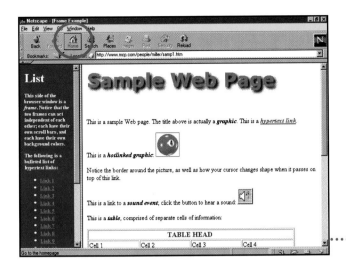

1 From any Web page, click the **Home** button.

2 Your browser automatically loads your home page. ■

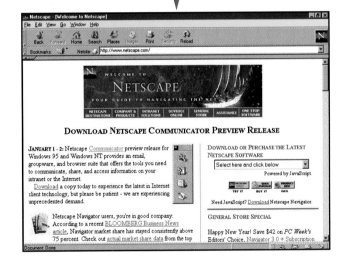

Missing Link

Most browsers come set with the manufacturer's home page as the default home page. For example, when you click the Home button in Netscape Navigator, the Netscape home page is loaded. However, you can change your browser's home page; see Task 18 for instructions.

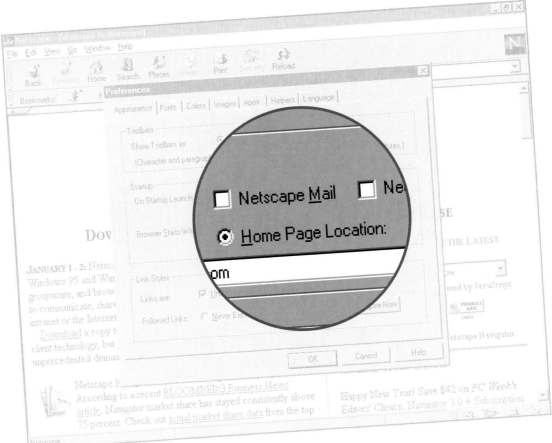

Setting Your Home Page

"Why would I do this?"

While you may be happy with your browser's default home page, many users prefer to choose the page that loads when they launch their browsers. You do this from your browser's Preferences or Options menu. If you want, you can even create a *custom start page*, personalized specifically for your needs. See Task 50 for instructions on how to create your own personal start page.

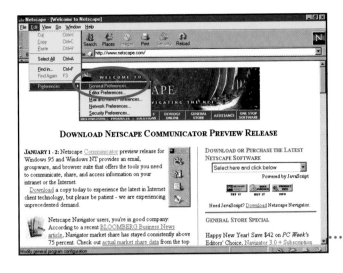

1 If you're using Netscape Navigator, pull down the **Edit** menu, select **Preferences**, and then select **General Preferences**.

2 When the Preferences dialog box appears, select the **Appearance** tab.

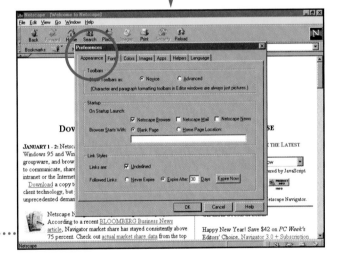

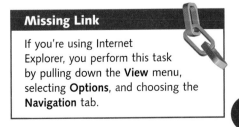

3 In the Startup section, select **Browser Starts with Home Page Location** and then enter the URL for your new home page in the text box below that. Click **OK** to finish the task. ■

Missing Link

If you're using Internet Explorer, you perform this task by pulling down the **View** menu, selecting **Options**, and choosing the **Navigation** tab.

Revisiting Your History

"Why would I do this?"

After you've visited several Web pages, you may want to return to a page you've already seen. To avoid retyping the URL, you can simply access the browser's *history* list to see a list of pages you've recently visited. If the page is listed there, you can return to it quickly.

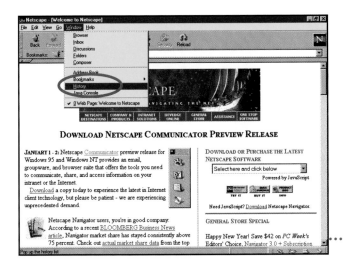

1 In Netscape Navigator, pull down the **Window** menu and select **History**.

2 When the History window appears, select the page you want to revisit and click the **Go to** button. The page you selected will be reloaded into your main browser window. ■

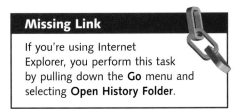

Missing Link

If you're using Internet Explorer, you perform this task by pulling down the **Go** menu and selecting **Open History Folder**.

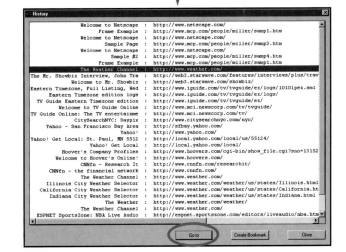

Keeping Track of Favorite Pages

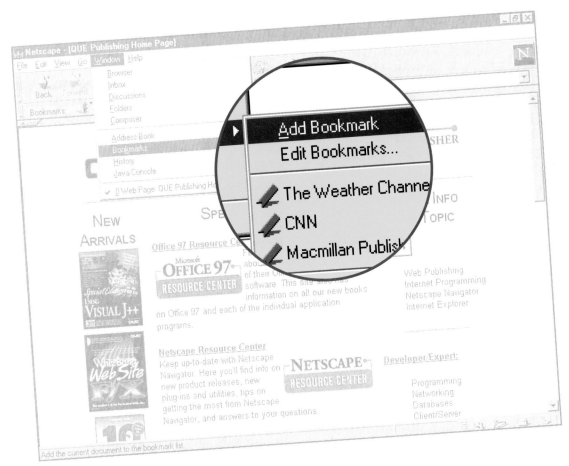

"Why would I do this?"

When you visit a Web page you like, you may want to *bookmark* it for future visits. A bookmark list (also called a *favorites* in Internet Explorer) is a list of your favorite pages. To visit a bookmarked page, you can just select it from the list instead of entering the complete URL.

You can easily add bookmarks to or delete bookmarks from your master bookmark list; you can also rearrange items within the list.

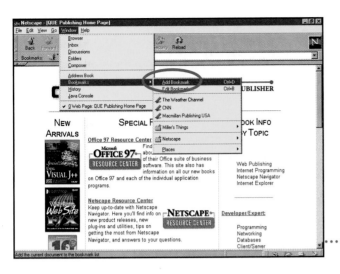

1 To add the current page as a bookmark, pull down the **Window** menu, select **Bookmarks**, and then choose **Add Bookmark**. The current page is added to your bookmark list.

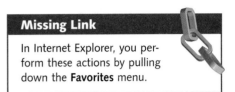

Missing Link

In Internet Explorer, you perform these actions by pulling down the **Favorites** menu.

2 To select a bookmark from your bookmark list, pull down the **Window** menu, select **Bookmarks**, and choose the page you want to visit. Your browser will automatically load the chosen page.

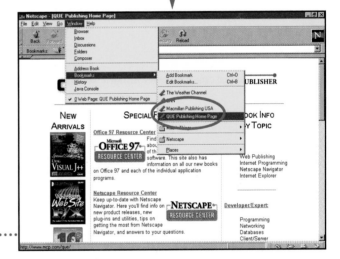

3 To edit your bookmark list, begin by pulling down the **Window** menu, selecting **Bookmarks**, and choosing **Edit Bookmarks**.

Task 20: Keeping Track of Favorite Pages

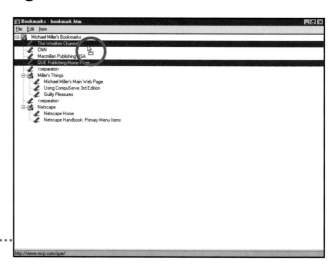

4 To move a bookmark up or down the list, select the bookmark with your mouse and drag it to the desired position.

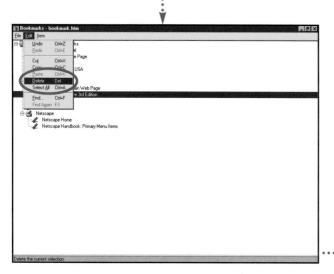

5 To remove an item from your bookmark list, select the item, pull down the **Edit** menu, and select **Delete**.

6 To insert a separator between two book-marks, select the bookmark that will be directly *above* the separator, pull down the **Item** menu, and select **Insert Separator**.

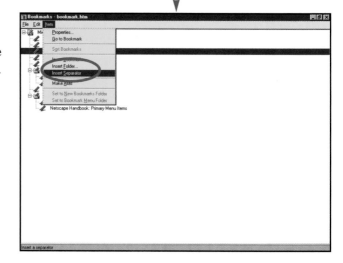

Missing Link

Bookmark-related tasks in Netscape Navigator can also be accomplished by pulling down the **Bookmarks** menu on the second tool-bar. Many tasks also have keyboard shortcuts; for example, you can add a bookmark by pressing **Ctrl+D** and edit the bookmark list by pressing **Ctrl+B**.

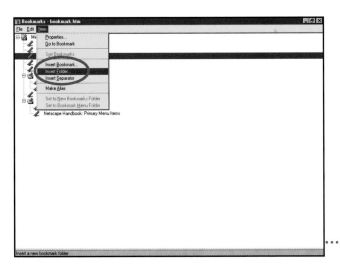

7 You can also subdivide your bookmark list by using *folders*. To add a folder, select the bookmark that will be directly *above* the new folder, pull down the **Item** menu, and select **Insert Folder**. When the Bookmark Properties dialog box appears, give the folder a name and click **OK**.

8 To add a bookmark to a folder, select the bookmark with your mouse and drag it to the folder. ■

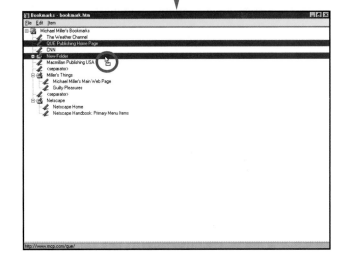

Missing Link

You can also copy a shortcut for a bookmark directly to your Windows 95 desktop. Position your cursor on any blank spot on the current page and click the *right* mouse button. When the pop-up menu appears, select **Internet Shortcut**, and the Create Internet Shortcut dialog box appears. Click **OK** to create an icon on your desktop; from then on, you can click the icon to launch your Web browser and load the selected page.

Printing a Web Page

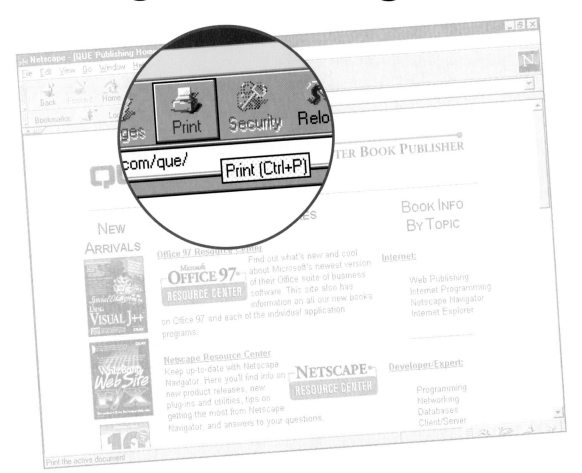

"Why would I do this?"

Sometimes you want a hard copy of a page you've visited. Fortunately, all computer-based browsers let you print a copy of any Web page. (However, WebTV does not presently have printing capability.)

Note that if you're printing a long Web page, it may print out over several sheets of paper.

1 After the page you're visiting has finished loading, click the **Print** button.

2 When the Print dialog box appears, make sure all settings are correct and click **OK**. The current page starts printing. ■

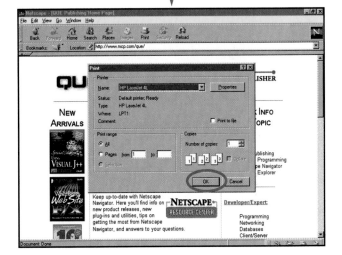

Missing Link

You can also save a copy of any Web page to your computer's hard disk. Just pull down the **File** menu and select **Save As**; the current Web page will be saved in HTML format to the location you specify on your hard disk.

PART V

Nine Ways to Search the Web

IF EVERYTHING IN THE WORLD eventually finds its way onto the Internet, how do you find any one thing? It's like finding a needle in a haystack. You know that what you want is there, but it's buried amidst millions of different Web pages, hidden in plain site yet virtually inaccessible—that is, unless you have a tool to effectively and efficiently search for it.

There are two types of tools on the Web to help you search for information: search engines and directories. Sometimes you'll find these tools referred to collectively as "search sites."

A *search engine* does just what it says—searches the Web for particular information. Most search engines, such as AltaVista, have cataloged millions of Web pages for your searching pleasure. But search engines don't record a lot of information about each page. So you'll get a big list of results, but very little information on any particular "hit."

A *directory* is a hand-picked list of Web sites. Most directories, such as Yahoo!, organize their lists of titles by topic and provide some sort of commentary about the sites. Because directories either use their own staff to add new pages to their lists or rely on user submissions, your search results won't be as exhaustive as what you get from a search engine—nor as up-to-date. You will, however, know more about each of the "hits" that result from your search request.

There are dozens of search sites on the Web. Some of these sites are devoted to specialized topics, such as financial or medical information. Other sites are more general, attempting to catalog as much of the Internet as they possibly can. Which search site you should use depends on what you're looking for and how much you know. The following table gives you some guidelines.

This section presents nine different search sites, including those listed in the table. These sites all work similarly, but each has its own unique quirks. I'll try to give you some tips on how to get the most out of each of these popular search engines and directories, such as:

- If you know exactly what you're looking for, search for that exact phrase. For example, if you're looking for information on the movie *Monty Python and the Holy Grail*, enter **monty python and the holy grail**. (Some search sites ask you to enclose exact phrases within quotation marks, as in **"monty python and the holy grail"**.)

- If you *don't* know exactly what you're looking for, enter a more general phrase or part of a phrase. For example, if you're looking for general information about Monty Python movies—including, but not limited to, *Monty Python and the Holy Grail*—enter **monty python movies**. If you're interested in *anything* about Monty Python, enter **monty python**; if you're not sure how to spell Python, just enter **monty**.

Note that most of these search sites offer additional features above and beyond simple searching, such as up-to-the-minute news feeds, custom mapping, and personalized start pages. I encourage you to browse the sites when you have some free time—you'll find some neat things there!

> **Missing Link**
>
> Because the Internet is an ever-changing medium, some of the Web sites and software you see in this book may differ from what you see on the Internet.

Choosing the Right Search Site

If You Are...	Try This Search Site
Looking for Web pages, and you're easily intimidated	Yahoo! (**http://www.yahoo.com**)
Looking for Web pages, and you're a sophisticated user	AltaVista (**http://www.altavista.digital.com**)
Looking for Web pages, and you can't decide between a directory and a search engine	Infoseek (**http://www.infoseek.com**)
Looking for personal Web pages from other users	Personal Seek (**http://www.personalseek.com**)
Looking for e-mail addresses	WhoWhere (**http://www.whowhere.com**)
Looking for street addresses and phone numbers	Switchboard (**http://www.switchboard.com**)
Looking for postings in UseNet newsgroups	DejaNews (**http://www.dejanews.com**)
Looking for files to download	Download.com (**http://www.download.com**)
Looking for FTP sites	Archie (**http://www-ns.rutgers.edu/htbin/archie**)
Looking for a specific type of information, and you have no idea where to look	Search.com (**http://www.search.com**)

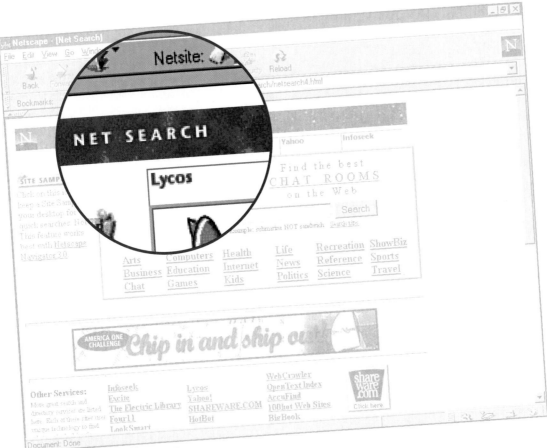

Searching the Web from Netscape Navigator

"Why would I do this?"

Five major search sites pay Netscape a hefty fee to be part of Netscape's NetSearch page. This NetSearch page appears when you click the Search button on Navigator's toolbar. From the NetSearch page, you enter the phrase you're searching for, and then select which of the five major search sites you want to use for your search. It's a great way to get started on your quest of searching the Internet!

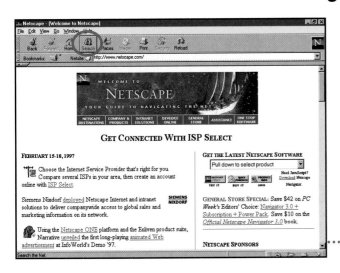

1 To display Netscape's NetSearch page, click the **Search** button on Navigator's toolbar.

2 Select the search site you want to use: Lycos, WebCrawler, Excite, Yahoo!, or Infoseek.

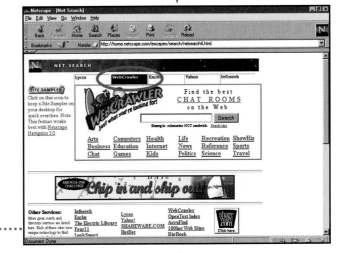

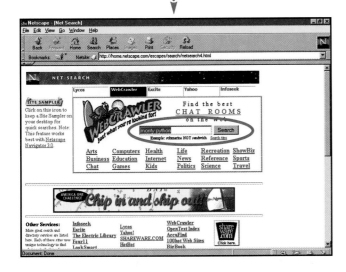

3 Enter your search phrase in the text box, and then click **Search**. For example, to search for "Monty Python," enter **monty python**. Your results appear on a new page; click any link to go directly to that page. ■

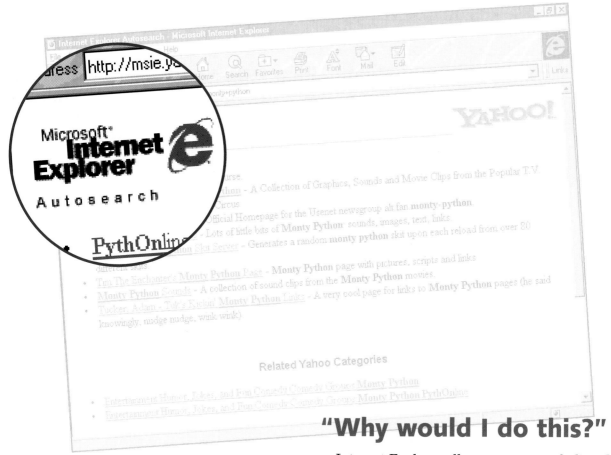

Searching the Web from Internet Explorer

"Why would I do this?"

Internet Explorer allows you to search directly from the main browser window. While this is a very convenient way to search, it limits you to the search engine selected by Microsoft. That search engine is a subset of the Yahoo! directory. You may want to start your searches from within Explorer and then move on to other search engines if you don't find what you're looking for.

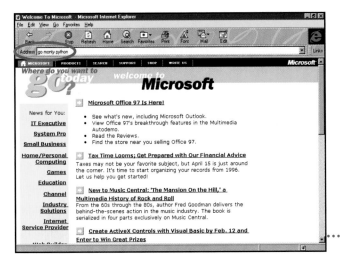

1 In the **Address** box, type **go**, followed by your search terms. For example, to search for "Monty Python," enter **go monty python**.

2 Internet Explorer's Autosearch uses a special version of Yahoo! and returns its results on a new page. Click any link to go directly to that page.

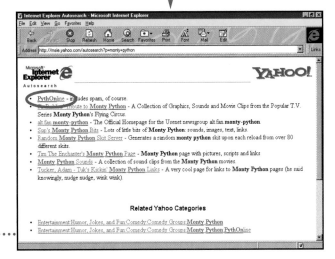

3 The Autosearch version of Yahoo! is smaller than the normal Yahoo! directory. To automatically search *all* of Yahoo!, scroll to the bottom of the Autosearch results page and click the **Search Yahoo!** button. ■

Searching the Web from WebTV

"Why would I do this?"

WebTV has partnered with the Excite search engine to provide customized search capabilities to WebTV subscribers. Excite is a good search engine, but you may want to explore other search engines if you don't find what you're looking for right away.

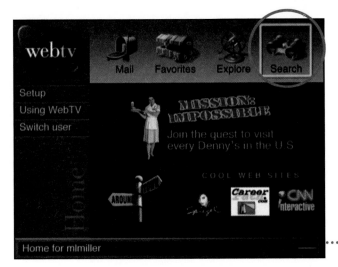

1 To begin a search, click the **Search** icon on the WebTV home page or press the **Search** button on the optional WebTV wireless keyboard.

2 The custom Excite search page appears. Enter your search term in the blank and click the **Search** button.

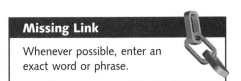

Missing Link

Whenever possible, enter an exact word or phrase.

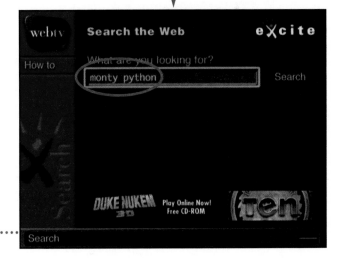

3 The results of your search are displayed on a new page. Click any link to go directly to that page, or scroll to the bottom of the page and click the **More Results** button to see more results. ■

TASK

25

Searching Search.com

"Why would I do this?"

If you don't know which search engine or directory to use, you might want to check out Search.com. This site, run by c|net, is essentially a "directory of directories," or what techies call a "metasearch" site. Use Search.com to look for the best search engine for your needs. It lists dozens of smaller, more topic-specific search engines and directories in addition to the normal large search sites.

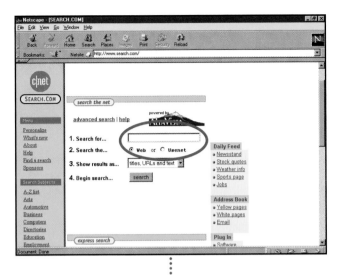

1 Go to the Search.com page at the following address:

http://www.search.com

From there you can use the "search engine of the day" to begin a direct search.

Missing Link

Search.com rotates search engines as the "search engine of the day." One day it may be AltaVista; another day it may be Yahoo!

2 Search engines arranged by subject are listed down the left side of the Search.com home page. Click **A-Z List** to see a complete alphabetical list of all available search engines.

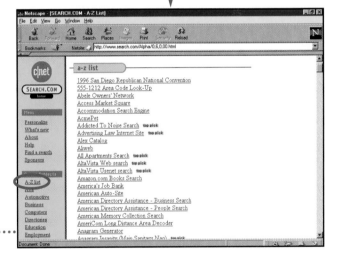

3 You can use Search.com to try to determine the right search engine for your specific needs by clicking **Find a Search**. Enter your search term in the blank to generate a list of the most appropriate search engines for your request.

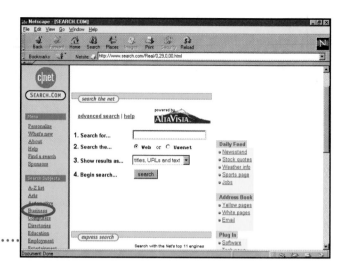

4 To view a list of all search engines in a particular category, click that category in the list. For example, click **Business** to see a list of all business-related search sites.

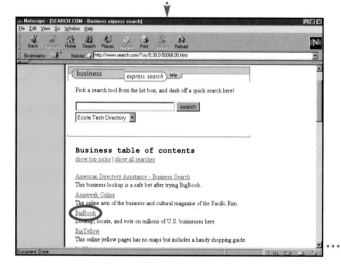

5 From the list of search engines within a given category, click a specific engine to begin your search. For this example, click **BigBook**.

6 Search.com displays a search form for the selected search site, without taking you directly to the site—or at least not yet. Fill in the blanks and click **Search** to begin your search.

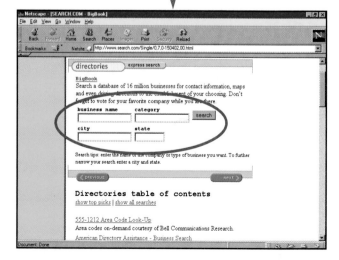

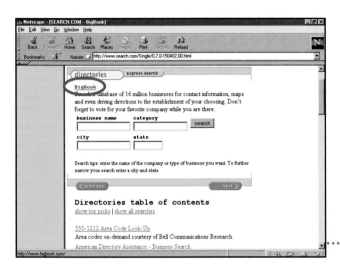

7 You can also click the search engine's name to go directly to the site, bypassing Search.com as a "middleman."

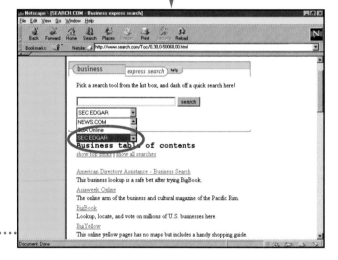

8 You also have the option of performing a "quick search" from the top of the search engine listing. Search.com selects a handful of the most popular engines for this list. Pull down the list box and choose a tool.

9 You're automatically taken to the chosen site, and the results of your search are displayed on-screen. ■

Searching Yahoo!

"Why would I do this?"

The most popular search site on the Web has a funny name with an exclamation point at the end: Yahoo! Technically, Yahoo! is not a search engine—it's a directory of Web sites. Yahoo! hand-picks sites for its directory, organizes the sites by category, and gives you the option of searching its directory for the sites you need.

1 Go to the Yahoo! home page at the following address:

http://www.yahoo.com

The easiest way to use Yahoo! is to click one of the listed categories. This normally gives you a more detailed list of subcategories; keep clicking subcategories until you find the listing of sites you want.

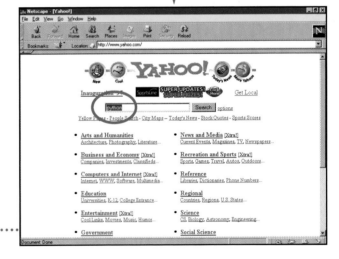

2 To search the Yahoo! site, enter a word in the text box and click the **Search** button.

3 Yahoo! automatically lists all sites that match your search term. Click a link to go directly to that site.

4 If you're searching for sites that contain a specific phrase, enclose the phrase in quotation marks. For example, to search for Monty Python, enter **"monty python"**.

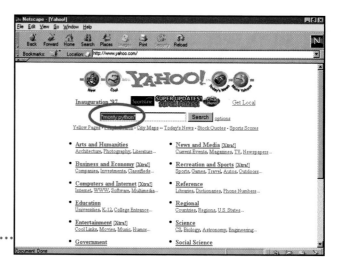

5 If you're searching for sites that *must* include a specific word, add a "**+**" before the word in the search blank. For example, to search for any monty that is definitely a python, enter **monty +python**.

6 If you're searching for sites that must *not* include a specific word, add a "**–**" before the word in the search blank. For example, to search for any monty *except* Monty Python, enter **monty –python**.

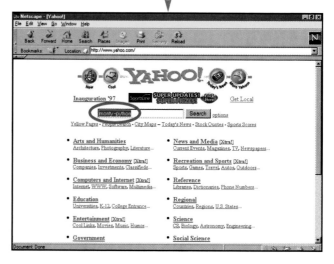

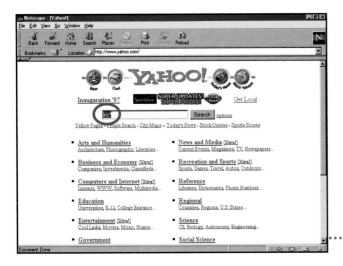

7 If you only know part of a word, enter the rest of the word as a "wild card" by using an asterisk (*). For example, to search for Rick, Rich, or Richard, enter **ric***.

8 To use more advanced search options, click **Options**.

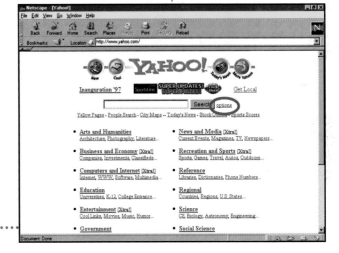

9 Use the Search Options page to customize your search. You can choose to search specific areas within Yahoo!, specify a particular search method, or search those listings created since a specific date. ■

Searching Lycos

"Why would I do this?"

Where Yahoo! is not a search engine (it's a directory), Lycos most definitely *is* a search engine. Lycos uses a special software program called a *spider* to roam the Web and catalog new pages and sites as they're created. The downside of Lycos (and other search engines) is that the sites listed are not qualified or organized in any way. The upside, of course, is that Lycos lists a lot more sites than does Yahoo! or any directory.

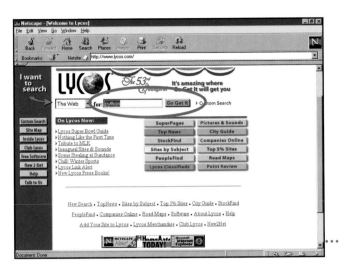

1 Go to the Lycos home page at the following address:

http://www.lycos.com

To begin a search, enter a word in the blank and click **Go Get It**.

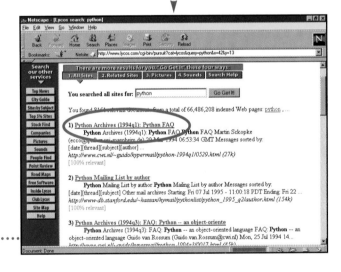

2 Lycos automatically lists all sites that match your search term. Click any link to go directly to that site.

3 If you're searching for sites that must *not* include a specific word, add a – before the word in the search blank. For example, to search for any monty *except* Monty Python, enter **monty –python**.

4 If you only know part of a word, enter the rest of the word as a "wild card" by using a dollar sign (**$**). For example, to search for Rick, Rich, or Richard, enter **ric$**.

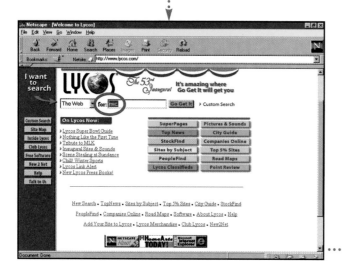

5 If you're searching for sites that *exactly* match a specific word, add a period (.) after the word. For example, to look for mic (and *not* Michael or microphone), enter **mic.** in the blank.

6 To use more advanced search options, click **Custom Search**.

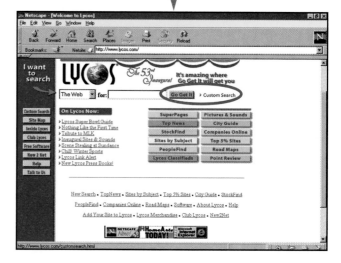

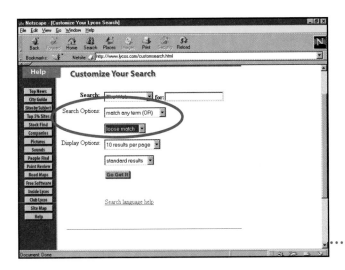

7 Use the Custom Search page to customize your search and display options. Then click **Go Get It**.

8 You can also use Lycos to search for sounds, pictures, or general subjects. Pull down the list box (which defaults to The Web) to choose an alternative search item.

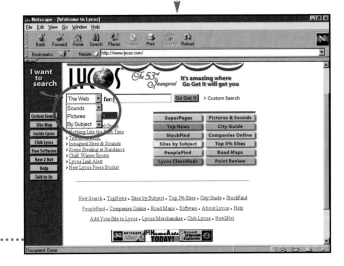

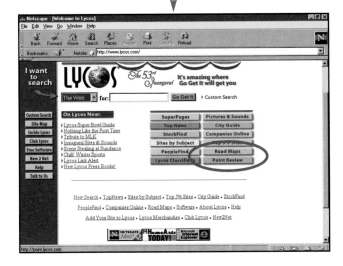

9 To read reviews of the top five percent of all Web sites, click **Point Review**. ■

TASK 28

Searching Infoseek

"Why would I do this?"

Like Yahoo!, Infoseek is a directory with Web sites that have been hand-picked for the listing. Unlike Yahoo!, Infoseek also includes a search engine, called Ultraseek, as part of its site. This means you get the best of both worlds—the hand-picked listings in the Infoseek directory and a much larger universe of sites with the Ultraseek search engine.

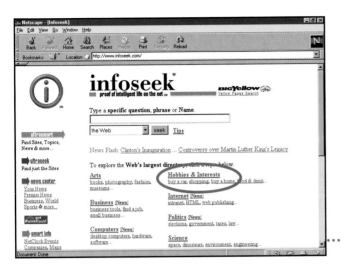

1 Go to the Infoseek home page at the following address:

http://www.infoseek.com

The easiest way to use Infoseek is to click one of the listed categories. This normally gives you a more detailed list of subcategories; keep clicking subcategories until you find the listing of sites you want.

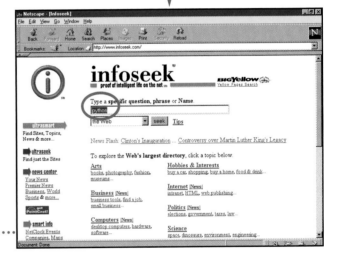

2 To begin a search of the Infoseek directory, enter a word in the blank and click **Seek**.

3 Infoseek automatically lists all sites that match your search term. Click any link to go directly to that site.

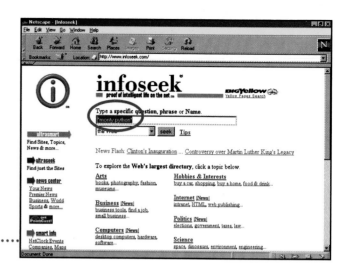

4 If you're searching for sites that contain a specific phrase, enclose the phrase in quotation marks. For example, to search for Monty Python, enter **"monty python"**.

5 If you're searching for sites that *must* include a specific word, add a plus sign (**+**) before the word in the search blank. For example, to search for any monty that is definitely a python, enter **monty +python**.

6 If you're searching for sites that must *not* include a specific word, add a minus sign (**–**) before the word in the search blank. For example, to search for any monty *except* Monty Python, enter **monty –python**.

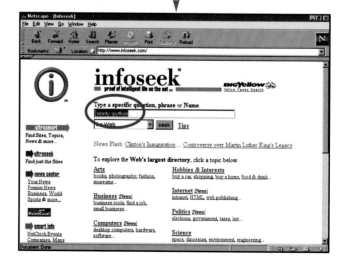

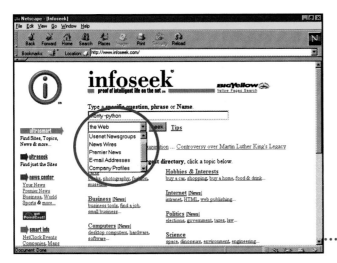

7 To search parts of the Internet other than the Web, pull down the list box (which defaults to The Web) and choose another area to search.

8 To engage the Ultraseek search engine, click **Ultraseek**.

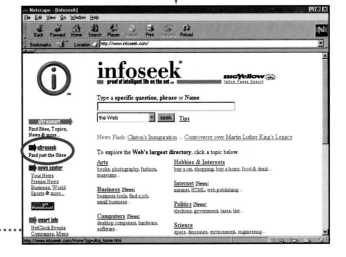

9 Ultraseek works just like Infoseek. Enter your search term in the blank, and then click **Seek**. The same search rules and conditions apply. ■

Searching AltaVista

"Why would I do this?"

AltaVista is the most popular search engine for the Web. Developed by the engineers at Digital Equipment Corporation, AltaVista is powered by numerous powerful DEC computers, which gives it a speed and breadth beyond its competitors. The downside of AltaVista is that it sometimes returns *too many* results; you often have to click through several pages of results to find the right one. But you'll get *more* results with AltaVista than with other engines; it's a definite case of quantity over quality.

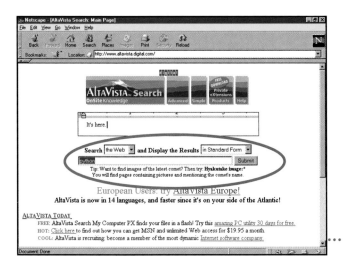

1 Go to the AltaVista home page at the following address:

http://www.altavista.digital.com

To begin a search, enter a word in the blank and click **Submit**.

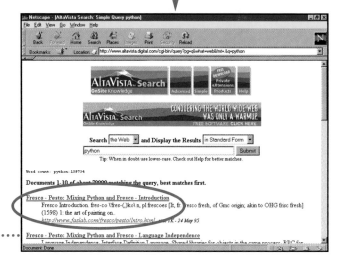

2 AltaVista automatically lists all sites that match your search term. Click any link to go directly to that site.

3 If you're searching for sites that contain a specific phrase, enclose the phrase in quotation marks. For example, to search for Monty Python, enter **"monty python"**.

4 If you're searching for sites that *must* include a specific word, add a plus sign (**+**) before the word in the search blank. For example, to search for any monty that is definitely a python, enter **monty +python**.

5 If you're searching for sites that must *not* include a specific word, add a minus sign (**–**) before the word in the search blank. For example, to search for any monty *except* Monty Python, enter **monty –python**.

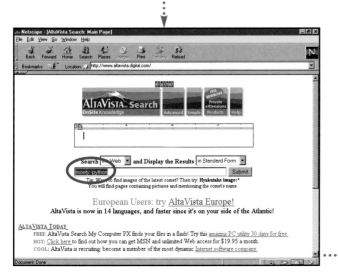

6 If you only know part of a word, enter the rest of the word as a "wild card" by using an asterisk (*****). For example, to search for Rick, Rich, or Richard, enter **ric***.

7 By default, AltaVista searches the Web, but it also lets you search UseNet newsgroups. To do so, pull down the list box (which defaults to The Web) and choose **Usenet** to search newsgroups.

8 To use more advanced search options, click **Advanced**.

9 The Advanced Query page lets you use more advanced syntax (such as the Boolean operators AND, OR, NOT, or NEAR) to further define your search. For example, to search for either Monty Clift *or* Monty Python, you would enter **monty AND clift OR python**. ■

Searching for Phone Numbers and Addresses

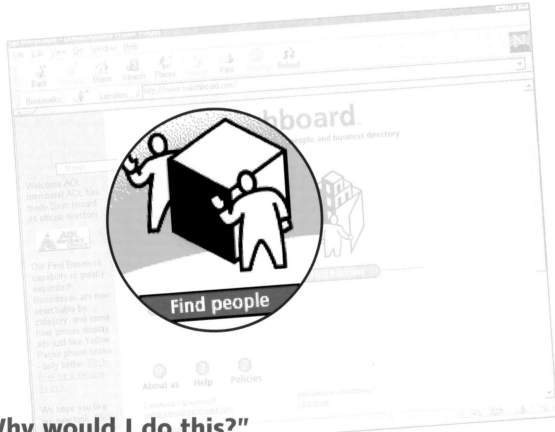

"Why would I do this?"

If you're looking for someone's address or phone number, there is no better place to look than on the Web. While you can use a normal Web search engine (like AltaVista) to search for people as well as pages, it's better to turn to a specialized "people finder," such as Switchboard.

Personally, I used Switchboard to locate some old school buddies just before my 20th high school reunion. It worked: I was able to contact several old friends and spend some quality time during the reunion!

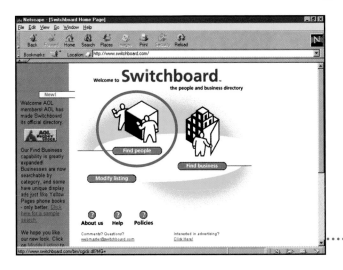

1 One of the best "people finders" on the Web is Switchboard. Go to Switchboard's home page at the following address:

http://www.switchboard.com

Click **Find People** to search for individual addresses and phone numbers.

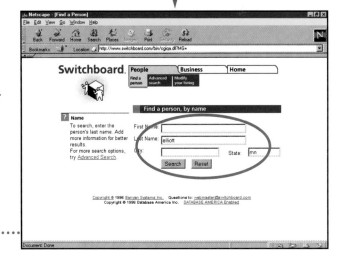

2 The more information you enter, the better the results will be. At the very least, enter a last name and a state (two-letter abbreviation, please). Then click **Search** to begin the search.

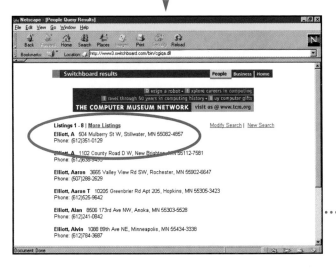

3 Switchboard automatically displays the closest matches to your request.

Puzzled?

If Switchboard *doesn't* list the person you're looking for, there may be several causes. You may need to make your search more general, like using an initial instead of a full first name. It's also possible that the person you're looking for doesn't live where you think anymore.

4 To search using a partial name, use a single letter. (Switchboard doesn't use "wild cards" like other engines.) For example, if you were to search for "S Elliott," your list of results would include "Sherry Elliot," "Sheryl Elliott," and "Susan Elliott."

5 To perform a more advanced search, click **Advanced Search**.

6 The advanced search option lets you search for individuals affiliated with certain organizations. It's a great way to find all members of a specific group.

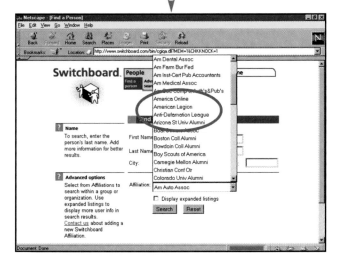

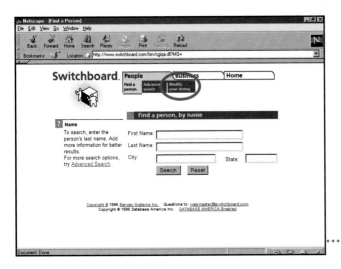

7 If you find that your own listing is incorrect, Switchboard lets you modify your personal listing. From the Switchboard home page, click **Modify Your Listing** and follow the on-screen instructions.

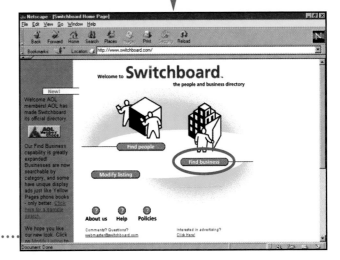

8 Switchboard also lets you search for businesses. From the Switchboard home page, click **Find Business**.

9 To find a specific business, select the business category and enter a city and state. Then click **Search**. ■

PART VI

Nine Web Sites for News and Information

WITH THE WORLD WIDE WEB, you can get just about all the news you want: current news headlines, in-depth topic analyses, specialized industry and company news, even news customized for your city or town. In fact, almost every major newspaper, magazine, and television news organization has a site on the Web, many of which offer more current news than you'll find in their other-media versions.

Information comes in various forms on the Web. Some sites just repackage their print news. Other sites offer a shorter, digest-like version of breaking stories. Still other sites offer more in-depth information online than they do in print.

The one thing that I like about getting my news, sports, and weather information online is that it's always up-to-date. Most news-based Web sites update their information constantly, so you can find out what's happening pretty much as it happens. There's no waiting around for the nightly news report, the morning newspaper, or the weekly newsmagazine.

A few of the sites (including CNN and ESPNET SportZone) let you create a "ticker" directly on your Windows 95 desktop. By clicking a button at these sites, you'll create a special window or icon that scrolls the latest news, scores, or stock reports automatically. (Note that these "tickers" are only updated while you're connected to the Web; when you break your connection, they can't update their information.)

My favorite information-related Web sites are CNN Online and The Weather Channel (I'm a news and weather junkie). There are lots of other sites available, however. The following table lists some of the most popular sites, arranged by category.

Missing Link

Because the Internet is an ever-changing medium, some of the Web sites and software you see in this book may differ from what you see on the Internet.

News and Information Sites on the Web

Web Site	Address
Entertainment	
E! Online	http://www.eonline.com
Entertainment Weekly	http://www.pathfinder.com/ew/
Mr. Showbiz	http://www.MrShowbiz.com
TV Guide Online	http://www.mci.newscorp.com/tv/
Financial	
CNNfn	http://cnnfn.com
Hoover's Online	http://www.hoovers.com
QuoteCom	http://www.quote.com
News	
Chicago Tribune	http://www.chicago.tribune.com
ClariNet	http://www.clarinet.com
CNN Online	http://www.cnn.com
Commercial News Services on the Internet (list)	http://www.jou.ufl.edu/commres/webjou.htm
Electronic Newsstand	http://www.enews.com
MSNBC	http://www.msnbc.com
USA Today	http://www.usatoday.com
Sports	
ESPNET SportsZone	http://espnet.sportszone.com
NBC Sports	http://www.nbc.com/sports/index.html
SportsLine USA	http://www.sportsline.com
XPC Sports	http://www.taponline.com/xpc/
Weather	
INTELLiCast	http://www.intellicast.com
National Weather Service	http://iwin.nws.noaa.gov/iwin/graphicsversion/main.html
The Weather Channel	http://www.weather.com

TASK 31

Visiting CNN Online for Current News

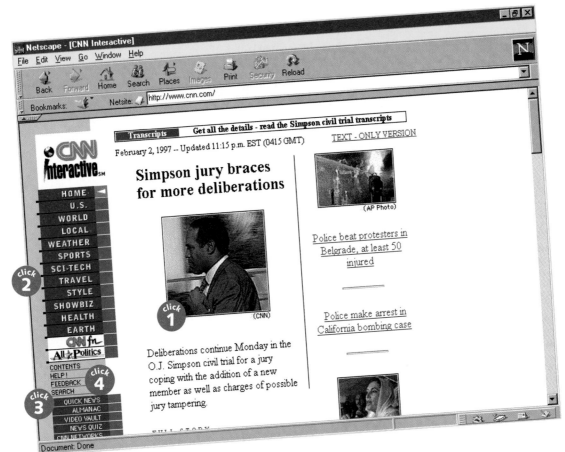

Go to CNN's main page at the following address: http://www.cnn.com

"Why would I do this?"

CNN is the main source for news on cable and satellite systems. It goes to figure that CNN would also be a powerful force in the online world—in fact, it's one of the best news sources on the Web. In addition, CNN also runs some related sites with more specialized information, such as CNNfn for financial news (see Task 34).

1 Click a story link to read the entire story. Many stories include additional links to related stories and background information.

2 Click a category to view all the current news in that category. On the category page, brief details of each story are listed; click **Full Story** to read the entire story. Scroll down to the bottom of the category page to see recent stories in the category.

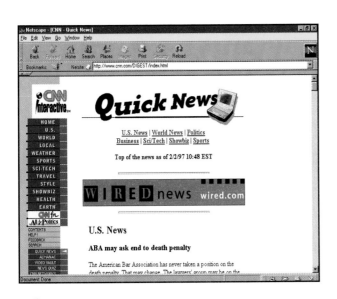

3 Click **Quick News** to view concise versions of today's most important stories (in an easy-to-read digest format). Stories are arranged by category; click **Full Story** to read an entire story.

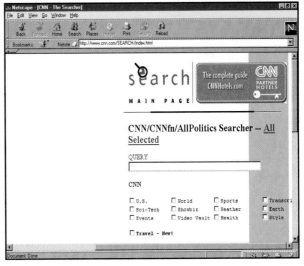

4 Click **Search** to search the CNN site for news about a specific subject. You can choose to search all of CNN's site (and the related CNNfn and AllPolitics sites), or just specific sections of the CNN site. Enter your search phrase in the **Query** box, and then click the **Begin the Search** button.

Visiting ESPN for Sports Information

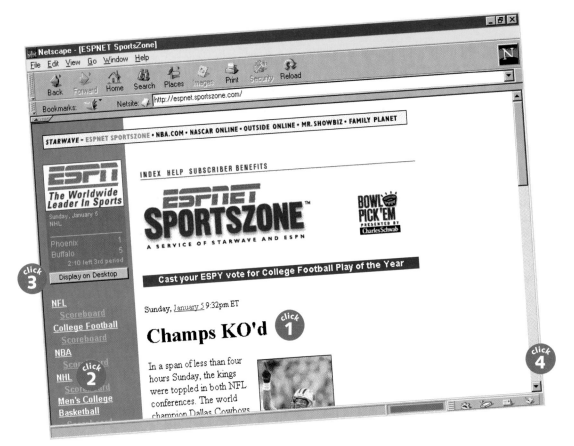

Go to ESPN's main page at the following address: http://espnet.sportszone.com

"Why would I do this?"

ESPN is available on the Web (as ESPNET SportsZone) with the latest scores and sports news. Note that parts of SportsZone are accessible only if you're a paid subscriber; however, all the scores and main news items are free to all users. SportsZone offers a great mix of scores and in-depth reporting—as well as information direct from ESPN's cable broadcasts.

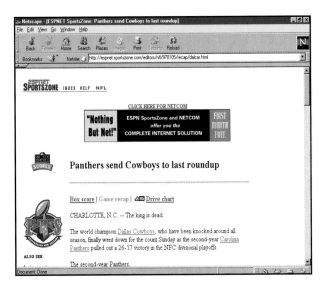

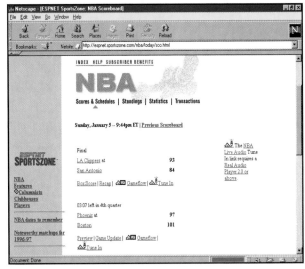

1 Click a story link to read the entire story. Many stories include links to video clips taken from ESPN broadcasts; click a link to watch the corresponding video on your PC.

2 To view current scores for a specific sport, click the sport's **Scoreboard** link. Many scoreboards include links for complete box scores, a concise game recap, an analysis of the gameflow, and (while the game is in progress) live audio play-by-play.

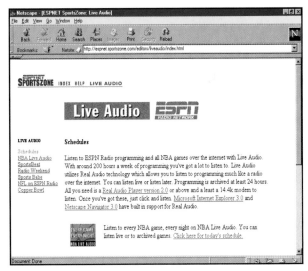

3 Add an up-to-the-minute sports ticker to your desktop by clicking the **Display on Desktop** button. This sports ticker stays on your desktop until you close it, and it is updated automatically as long as your Internet connection is open.

4 To hear live broadcasts of various sporting events over your PC's speakers, scroll down and click the **Live Audio** link. (Live Audio, like several other SportsZone features, is available only to paid subscribers.)

TASK 33

Visiting The Weather Channel for Current Forecasts

"Why would I do this?"

Go to The Weather Channel's main page at the following address:
http://www.weather.com

There are lots of weather-related resources on the Web, but the big daddy of them all is The Weather Channel. Utilizing the same resources as the popular cable network, The Weather Channel's online version offers national maps and forecasts, local forecasts for thousands of towns and cities across the U.S., and breaking weather news and information.

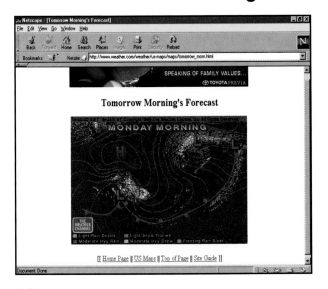

1 To view condition and forecast maps, click **The Weather**. Then click **U.S. Maps** and select the forecast map you want to see. The site offers maps that display satellite information, local and national radar, travel conditions, and so on.

2 To view local forecasts, select a state from the drop-down list, click the **Go State** button, and then click a specific city. Each local page includes four-day forecasts, as well as links to local weather radar.

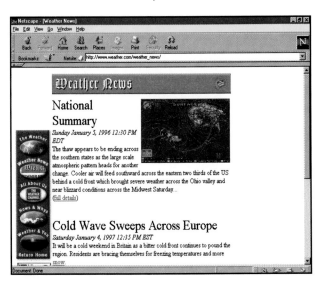

3 Read about the latest weather events by clicking **Weather News**. This is the place to turn to for news about severe storms, natural disasters, and the like.

4 Find out about potential flight delays by clicking **Weather and You** and selecting **Travel Weather**. You'll get a list of delays from many major airports.

Visiting CNNfn for Financial News

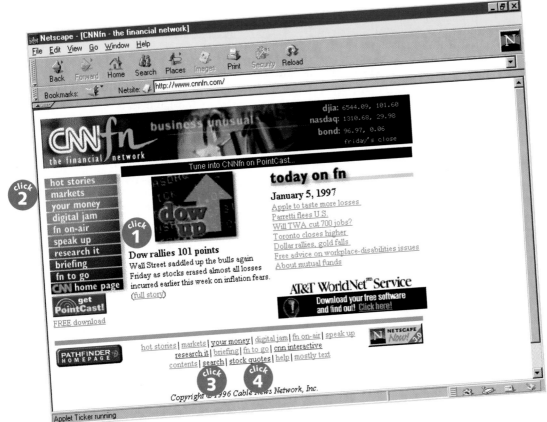

Go to CNNfn's main page at the following address: http://www.cnnfn.com

"Why would I do this?"

CNNfn is CNN's cable cousin, specializing in financial news and information. Just as CNN Online is the premiere Web site for general news, CNNfn is the premiere Web site for financial news. Look here for all your market information, including in-depth financial reporting, personal finance news, research information, and current stock quotes.

① Click a story link to read the entire story. Many stories include links to related stories and more in-depth information.

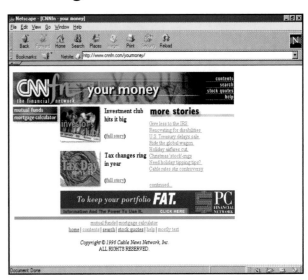

② Click a category to view all the news for that category. CNNfn lists the headlines for each category; click a headline to read the whole story.

③ Click **Search** to search the site for news on a specific company or topic. Enter your search term, select the area of CNNfn you want to search, and then click **Begin the Search**.

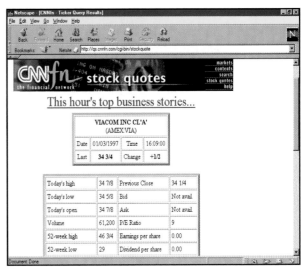

④ Click **Stock Quotes** to access the Stock Quotes page. You can receive current quotes for stocks, mutual funds, and money market funds. Enter one or more ticker symbols in the box (separated by spaces). Then click **Get quote**.

TASK

35

Visiting Hoover's Online for Investment Information

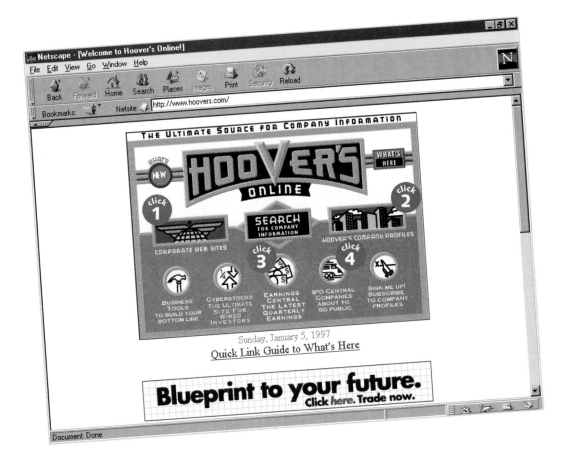

Go to Hoover's main page at the following address: http://www.hoovers.com

"Why would I do this?"

Hoover's offers company reports, financial information, addresses of corporate Web sites, and a database of job listings. (Note that some Hoover's reports and services are only available for a fee; for example, when you subscribe to Hoover's Company Profiles service, you get access to 100 profiles for $9.95/month.)

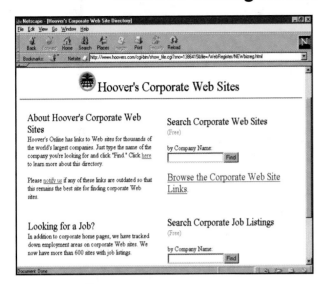

1 To search a database of more than 4,000 Web sites from individual companies, click **Corporate Web Sites**. This page also lets you search a database of corporate job listings, compiled from more than a thousand different Web sites.

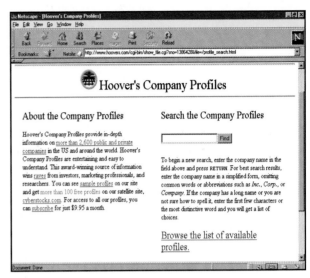

2 To obtain detailed reports on individual companies, click **Hoover's Company Profiles.** Hoover's provides profiles on more than 2,700 private and public companies.

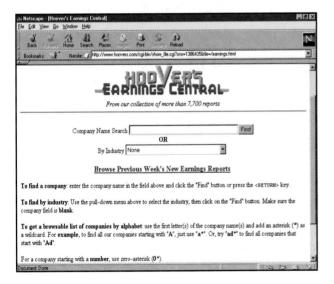

3 To read the latest quarterly earnings report for a specific company, click **Earnings Central.** You can search for companies via company name, ticker symbol, or industry.

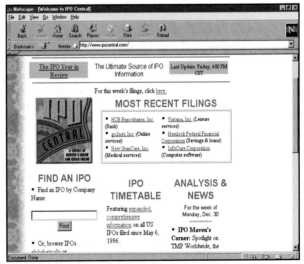

4 To get more information on companies about to go public, click **IPO Central**. IPO Central includes news on recent filings, performance evaluation of past initial public offerings, and general information about the IPO market.

Visiting TV Guide Online
for Television News

Go to TV Guide's main page at the following address: http://www.tvguide.com/tv/

"Why would I do this?"

The entire contents of TV Guide's print version are online at this site. In addition, there is a lot more information, and you can even exchange messages with your favorite television celebrities. TV Guide Online is part of the TV Guide Entertainment Network, which includes information on movies, music, sports, and other entertainment media.

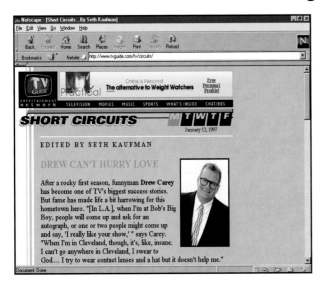

1 Click a link or picture to read the entire story. TV Guide Online often features different stories from those in the print edition. And many of the stories include links to audio clips from celebrity interviews.

2 Click **The Best TV Listings Anywhere** to access the traditional TV Guide program guide. You'll have to register (at no charge) and enter your ZIP code; then you'll see a grid of shows for your region.

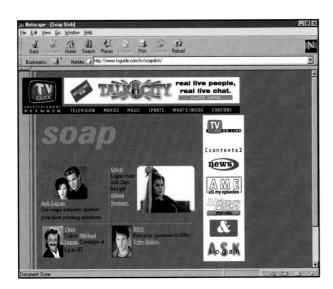

3 Get soap opera updates by clicking **Soap Dish**. Click **All My Episodes** to view synopses from all the major daytime soaps; click **News** for the latest soap-industry news.

4 Click the **TV Guide** logo to go to the larger, more comprehensive TV Guide Entertainment Network site, which includes Movie, Music, and Sports sections. The TV Guide Entertainment Network also includes a comprehensive movie database, complete with cast, credits, and reviews of more than 30,000 films.

TASK 37

Visiting Mr. Showbiz for Entertainment News

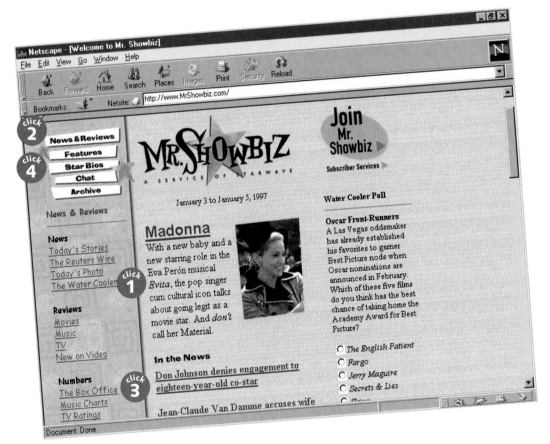

Go to the main Mr. Showbiz page at the following address:

http://www.MrShowbiz.com

"Why would I do this?"

While you can find print versions of *Entertainment Weekly* and other similar magazines, the best Web site for entertainment news has no magazine affiliation. *Mr. Showbiz* is a great site for all sorts of entertainment information, from celebrity interviews to weekly box office reports. New stories are posted every few days, so remember to check back frequently.

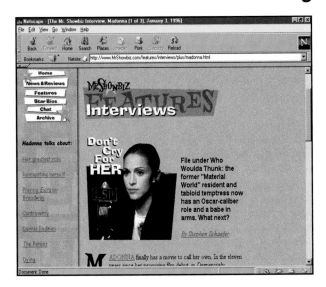

1 Click a link or picture to read the entire story. Many stories include links to related stories or background information on featured celebrities.

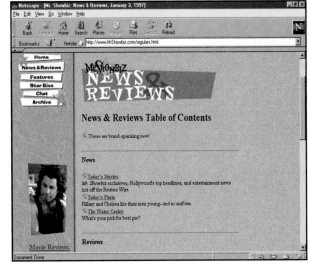

2 Click **News and Reviews** for up-to-the-minute show business news, as well as television and movie reviews and today's featured photo.

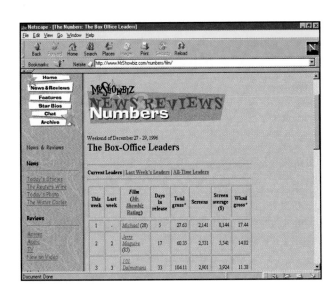

3 Click **The Box Office** to see which films led the box office last weekend. Mr. Showbiz also includes bestseller charts for music, television, and books.

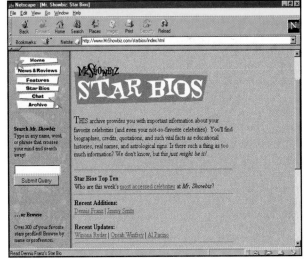

4 Click **Star Bios** to access an archive of information about major entertainment figures. A typical biography includes birthdate, birthplace, education, film/television credits, and links to related stories.

 38

Visiting Lycos City Guide for Local Information

"Why would I do this?"

Go to the City Guide San Francisco page at the following address:
http://cityguide.lycos.com/west/ SanFranciscoCA.html

With the advent of so-called local Web sites, residents can search for nearby businesses, and travelers can find out all about their destinations without leaving home. One of the best collections of local sites is City Guide, from Lycos. Go to **http://cityguide.lycos.com** to access local pages for more than 400 U.S. cities. (For the following example, I'll take you directly to the City Guide page for San Francisco.)

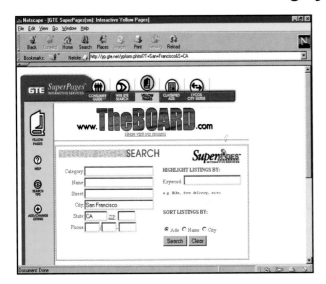

1 Click **Yellow Pages** to search for local businesses. You can search either by the name of a specific business or by general business category.

2 Click **People Find** to search for addresses and phone numbers of local residents. Enter the resident's last name (and first name, if you know it). Then click **Go Get It**. You can also use People Find to search for residents' e-mail addresses.

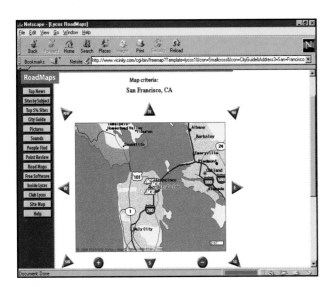

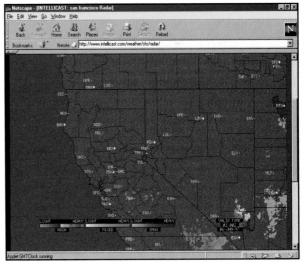

3 Click **Road Maps** to see a zoomable map of the area. Lycos automatically displays a total city map; click **New Location** to enter a specific street address and display a more localized map.

4 To view the local weather, click one of the topics under **Weather Report.** For San Francisco, Lycos displays radar maps, wind pattern maps, and current earthquake information.

Creating a Local Home Page with Yahoo! Get Local!

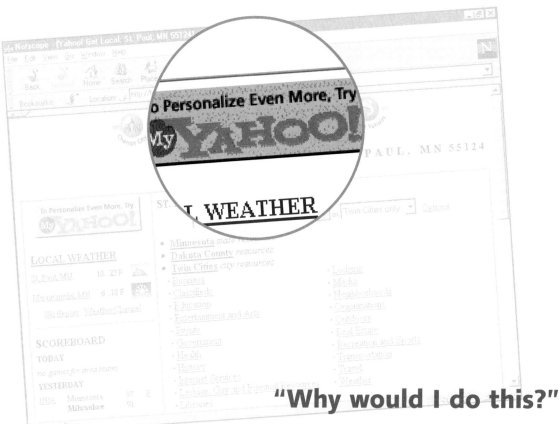

"Why would I do this?"

Yahoo! Get Local! lets you create a custom start page that includes local information for your city or town. The page is created automatically; all you have to do is enter your ZIP code, and Get Local! creates a Web page with all sorts of local links, weather reports, sports scores, and similar information.

1 Go to the main Yahoo! Get Local! page at the following address: **http://local.yahoo.com/local/**.

2 The fastest way to get your local page is via ZIP code (although you can also browse and select your state and city). Enter your five-digit ZIP code in the ZIP code box.

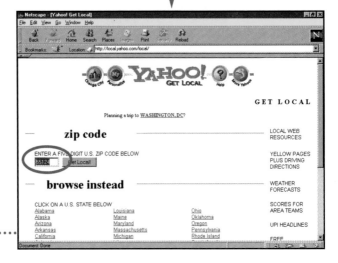

3 Click the **Get Local!** button, and Yahoo! creates a page full of localized information and resources for your specific location. ■

Missing Link

Yahoo! also offers hundreds of local pages for many cities and towns. Go to Yahoo's main page (**http://www.yahoo.com**) and click the **Regional:U.S.States** link to see if your city is listed.

129

PART VII

Seven Web Sites for Children and Families

THE WORLD WIDE WEB IS A GREAT PLACE for all sorts of information, as well as a lot of fun and games. This is especially true if you're looking for sites for your children or sites to help you with various family matters.

What do kids like to do online? For starters, kids like to do a lot of the same things adults do: search for information, get the latest news, and communicate with other online users. So some of the more popular kids sites are kid-specific directories (such as Yahooligans! at **http://www.yahooligans.com**), newspapers (such as KidNews at **http://www.vsa.cape. com/~powens/Kidnews3.html**), and chat sites (such as International Cool Kids, at **http:// cybercs.iserver.com/ick/**). Kids also like to play games and have fun—and there are lots of games-oriented sites just waiting for them.

There are also lots of sites for parents on the Web. Whether you're looking for health-related information or you just want to talk to some other parents online, the Web can be a good resource when you need a little help raising your children.

One of the great things about the Web's family-oriented sites is that they encourage participation from users. For example, many of the kids' sites feature content created by kids. And many of the family sites feature active discussion groups where you can get answers to your questions from both experts and other users.

The Web is also a great place for your children to do research for their homework, projects, and papers. There are several encyclopedias on the Web, as well as a variety of library and research sites. In addition to the sites mentioned in this section, make sure you check out Part 5, "Nine Ways to Search the Web," when your children are searching for information online.

In the tasks in this section, I'll review seven of the most popular sites for children and families. Addresses for even more family-oriented Web sites are listed in the following table.

Play It Safe

Don't forget that there are parts of the Web that you probably don't want your kids to visit. For that reason, you should check out some of the content filtering software, such as SurfWatch and Cyber Patrol (refer to Task 4). These programs work with your Web browser to block access to sites that have questionable content.

Web Sites for Children and Families

Web Site	Address
Berit's Best Sites for Children	http://www.cochran.com:80/theosite/ksites.html
Britannica Online	http://www.eb.com
Nye Labs (Bill Nye, the Science Guy)	http://nyelabs.kcts.org
Daily Parent	http://www.dailyparent.com
Disney.com	http://www.disney.com
EarlyChildhood.com	http://www.earlychildhood.com
Electric Library	http://www.elibrary.com
Family Health	http://www.tcom.ohiou.edu/familyhealth.html
Family.com	http://www.family.com
FamilyWeb	http://www.familyweb.com
GameKids	http://www.gamekids.com
Internet Health Resources	http://www.ihr.com
KidNews	http://www.vsa.cape.com/~powens/Kidnews3.html
kidsDoctor	http://www.kidsdoctor.com
KidSource	http://www.kidsource.com
KidSpace	http://www.kids-space.org
My-Kids	http://www.my-kids.com
My Virtual Reference Desk	http://www.refdesk.com
Nickelodeon	http://www.nick.com
Parent Soup	http://www.parentsoup.com
ParenthoodWeb	http://www.parenthoodweb.com
Parents Place	http://www.parentsplace.com
ParentTime	http://pathfinder.com/ParentTime/
Seussville (Dr. Seuss)	http://www.seussville.com
World Wide Web School Registry	http://web66.coled.umn.edu/schools.html
Yahooligans!	http://www.yahooligans.com

Searching for Kids' Sites with Yahooligans!

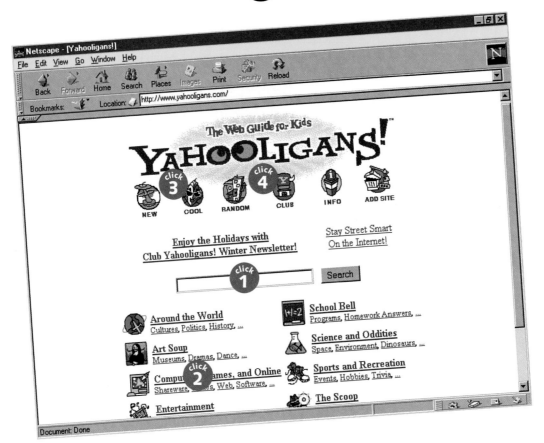

Go to the Yahooligans! main page at the following address:
http://www.yahooligans.com/

"Why would I do this?"

There are thousands of sites for children on the World Wide Web. Wouldn't it be nice to find a list of these sites all in one place? Fortunately, that place exists—as a part of the popular Yahoo! directory. Yahooligans! is a Yahoo! directory for kids, listing kid-friendly sites in a variety of categories.

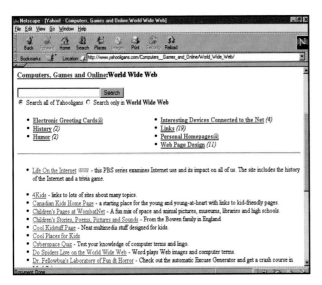

1 To search for a topic or site, enter a search phrase in the text box and click the **Search** button. The results appear on a separate page, organized by category.

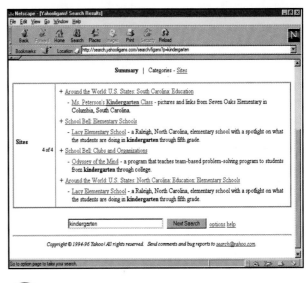

2 Click a topic from one of these categories: Around the World; Art Soup; Computers, Games, and Online; Entertainment; School Bell; Science and Oddities; Sports and Recreation; and The Scoop.

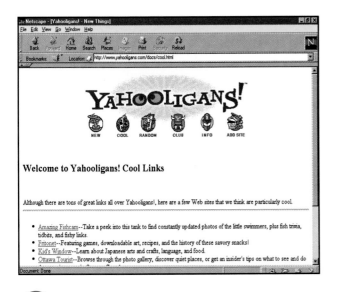

3 Click **Cool** to see a list of sites that the creators of Yahooligans! think are especially cool. You'll find twenty or so links to some of the best and most popular kids' sites on the Web.

4 Click **Club** to join Club Yahooligans! and receive regular e-mail updates that include sneak previews of cool sites, contests, and special offers.

Visiting KidSpace

Go to the KidSpace main page at the following address:

http://www.kids-space.org/

"Why would I do this?"

KidSpace is a unique site that lets your children interact with other children on the Web through stories, pictures, and songs. Children can submit their own works for browsing on the KidSpace site, as well as view works submitted by other children.

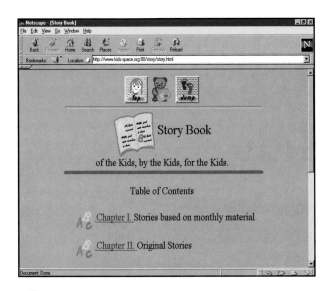

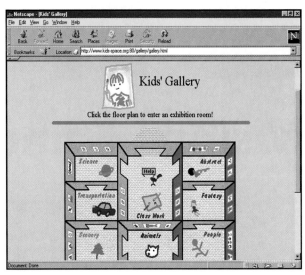

1   Click the storybook to go to the Story Book page, where you can read stories from other children. To submit a story of your own, scroll to the bottom of the Story Book page and click one of the **Submit** buttons.

2   Click the easel to go to the Kids' Gallery page, where you can view pictures from other users or submit pictures of your own. The Gallery is divided into several different rooms, each devoted to pictures on specific topics.

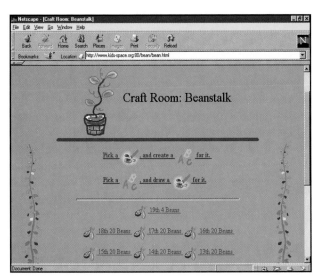

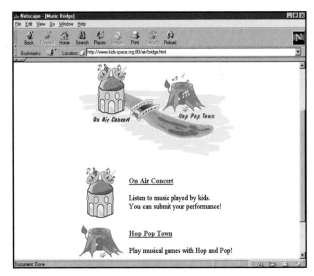

3   Click the beanstalk to go to the Craft Room page, where you can submit stories and pictures inspired by what you view in Story Book or Gallery. You can choose to draw a picture about a specific story or to write a story about a specific picture.

4   Click the music bridge to go to the Music Bridge page. From this page you can choose On Air Concert (where you can hear songs played by other users) or Hop Pop Town (where you can play musical games).

Visiting GameKids

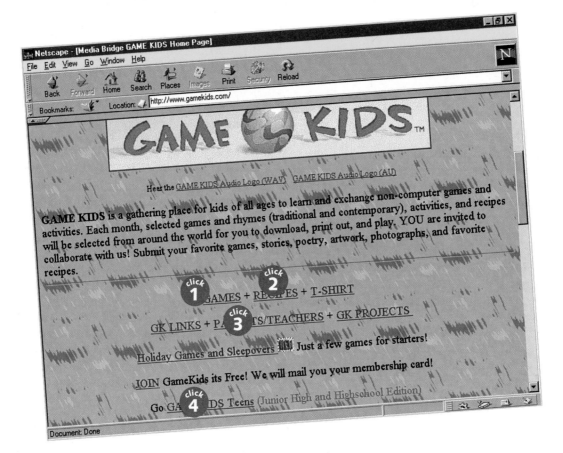

Go to the GameKids main page at the following address:
http://www.gamekids.com

"Why would I do this?"

Kids like to play games—it's as simple as that. GameKids is a site for both younger children and teenagers that focuses on participation games (the non-electronic kind) and other activities.

If your kids are more into electronic and online games, check out Task 49, "Playing Games on the Web."

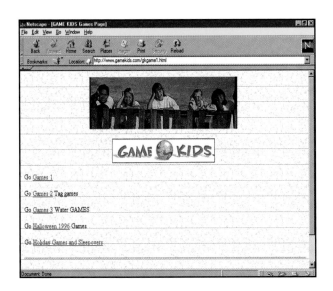

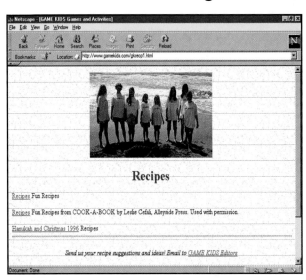

1 Click **GAMES** to access a variety of games for kids. You'll find all kinds of games—tag games, water games, holiday-related games, and more.

2 Click **RECIPES** to access an online cook-book full of recipes for and by kids. (Check here frequently; new recipes are constantly being posted!)

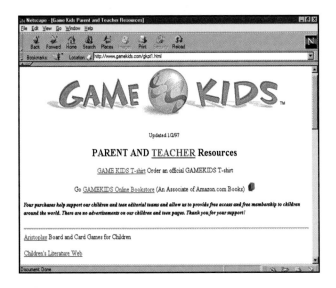

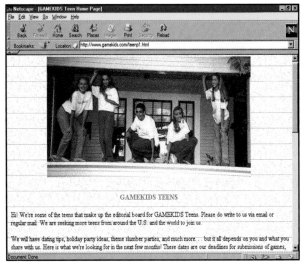

3 To access a list of resources for parents and teachers, click **PARENTS/TEACH-ERS**. Included are links to lots of good parenting and education Web sites.

4 Click **GAMEKIDS Teens** to access a site specifically for teen-agers. Here you'll find games and other activities for teens, including a special Web-based fashion show!

Visiting Britannica Online

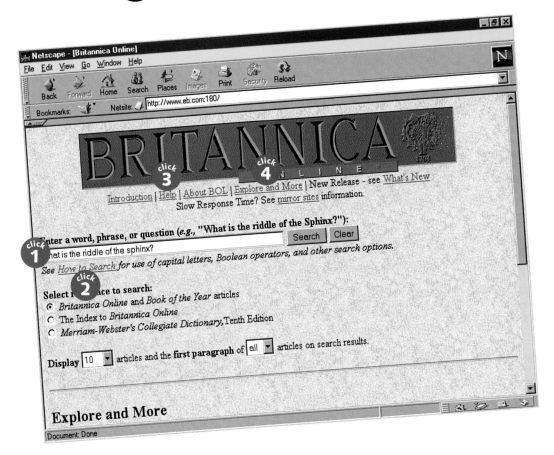

Go to the main page for Britannica Online at the following address:

http://www.eb.com

"Why would I do this?"

When it's homework time, you can direct your children to the big multi-volume print encyclopedia, or you can help them browse through an online encyclopedia. Britannica Online is great for doing homework or other research. Note, however, that it is a fee-based Web site: You pay $14.95/month or $150 for a yearly subscription. The first time you visit, you can either subscribe or choose a free seven-day trial; on subsequent visits, you'll go directly to the page shown here.

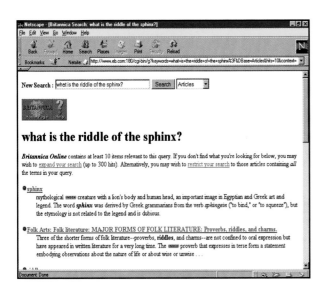

1 To search Britannica Online, enter a phrase in the text box, select the reference to search, and click **Search**. Britannica Online returns a list of articles that fit your query. Click an article's header to read the entire article.

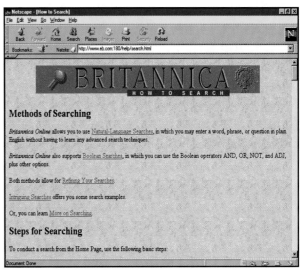

2 For more details on how to search Britannica Online, click **How to Search**. The page that appears next includes information on how to perform Boolean and other advanced searches.

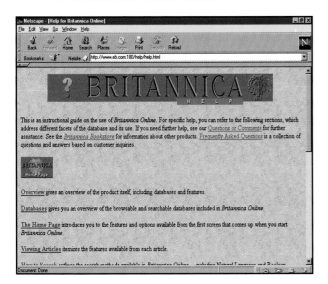

3 Click **Help** for complete instructions on how to use Britannica Online. You'll see a page from which you can choose to read an overview, learn more about Britannica Online's databases, explore all the features of the service, or work through a tutorial on how to search Britannica Online.

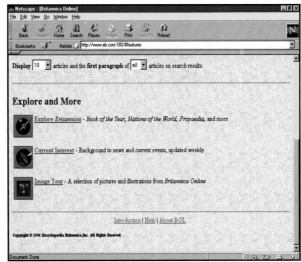

4 For more features, click **Explore and More**. From here, you can explore other features of Britannica Online (including Book of the Year and Nations of the World), get background information on current events, and browse a selection of pictures and illustrations from Britannica Online.

TASK

44

Visiting America's HouseCall Network

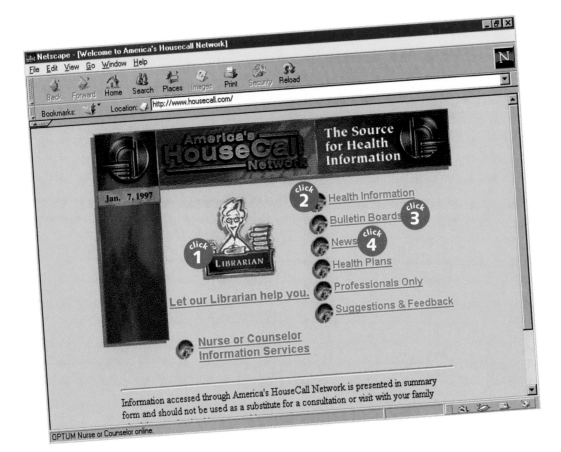

Go to the main page of America's HouseCall Network at the following address:

http://www.housecall.com/

"Why would I do this?"

America's HouseCall Network offers a variety of prepackaged information on common ailments, the ability to search its online database, and access to numerous "bulletin boards" where you can exchange messages with other users about various health topics. It's a good place to find answers to most of your questions about family health.

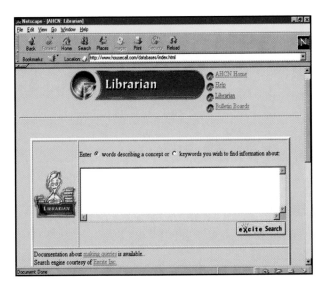

1 Click the librarian to go to the Librarian page, where you can search the online database for specific health topics.

2 Click **Health Information** to get information on specific ailments.

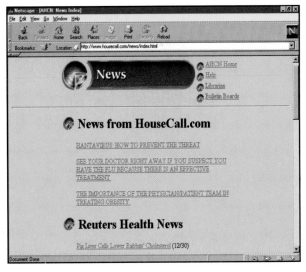

3 Click **Bulletin Boards** to exchange messages about various health issues with other users.

4 Click **News** to get the latest health news and bulletins.

Visiting Family.com

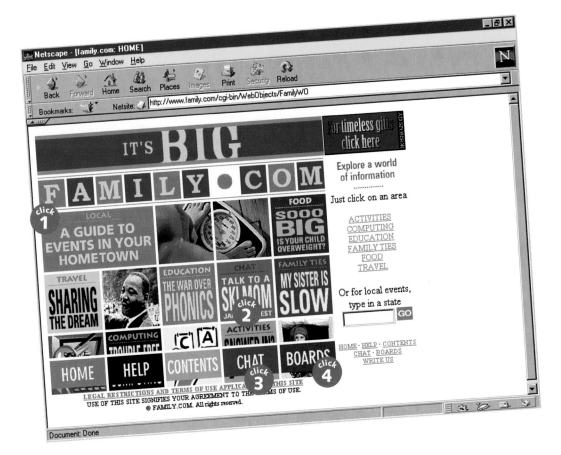

Go to the Family.com main page at the following address:

http://www.family.com

"Why would I do this?"

Family.com is a great resource for Web-savvy parents. Family.com connects hundreds of local family-related newspapers and magazines, so there are lots of local links and information available. It's all yours, just for the clicking.

1 Click **LOCAL** to view a list of family-related events and Web links in your area. Local publications are listed by state. Click the appropriate links to go directly to local information and events.

2 Click **ACTIVITIES** for stories on things to do with your family. The Activities page also includes a search engine that lets you search for types of activities by age group.

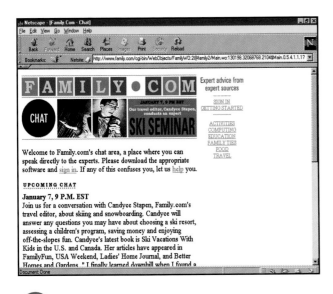

3 Click **CHAT** to participate in specially scheduled conferences with parenting experts. These conferences are like big group chat sessions with featured guests. Note also that the conferences are generally moderated to facilitate a more orderly session.

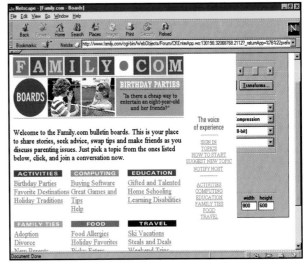

4 Click **BOARDS** to exchange messages with other users on a variety of family-related topics. Top-level bulletin board topics include Activities, Computing, Education, Family Ties, Food, and Travel.

Visiting Parent Soup

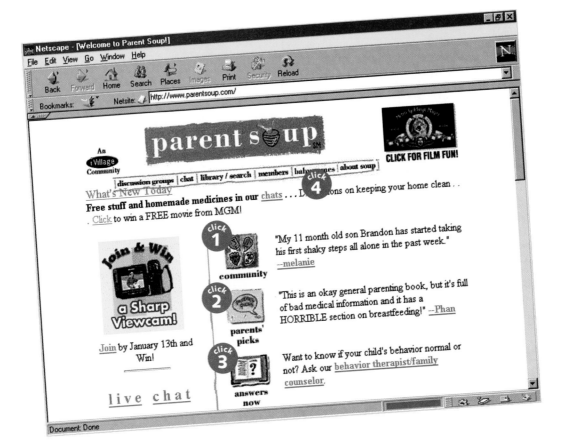

Go to the Parent Soup main page at the following address:
http://www.parentsoup.com

"Why would I do this?"

Parent Soup has a lot of great content—most of which is provided by other parents, just like yourself. I especially like the reviews of toys, books, and movies provided by other parents. And for you soon-to-be parents, check out the "online baby name finder." It'll help you find just the right name for your child.

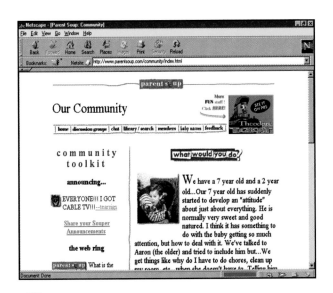

1 Click **Community** to communicate with other parents in the Parent Soup "community." There are three different communities: one for parents of babies and toddlers, one for parents of five- to eleven-year olds, and one for parents of teens.

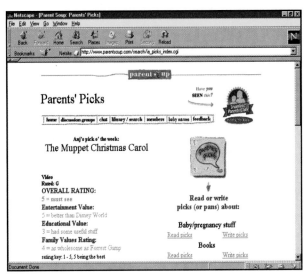

2 Click **Parents' Picks** to read reviews from other users, including reviews of books, movies, toys, and computer software. You can also add your own reviews to the Parents' Picks section.

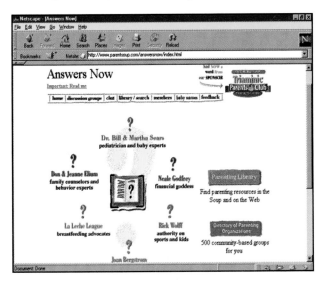

3 Click **Answers Now** to ask questions of experts in a variety of fields. Parent Soup features pediatrician and baby experts, breastfeeding experts, education experts, family counselors, and behavior therapists.

4 Click **Baby Names** for an online baby name finder. Here you can search for baby names from Aaron to Zuriel—and even join a baby names discussion group!

PART VIII

Six Other Things to Do on the Web

THIS SECTION INCLUDES SIX very different tasks that illustrate some of the other things you can do on the Web. These tasks include:

- **Making Travel Plans.** There are literally hundreds of different Web sites offering travel-related information; many of these sites also let you book your own flight and hotel reservations. It's really convenient to book your travel online. You can find out what's available and for what cost, and then confirm everything right from home.

Many sites (such as MapQuest, at **http://www.mapquest.com**) also let you create a map of your destination.

My favorite travel sites are TravelWeb (described in Task 47), Travelocity (**http://www.travelocity.com**), Microsoft's Expedia (**http://www.expedia.msn.com**), and Macmillan's own Arthur Frommer's Outspoken Encyclopedia of Travel (**http://www.frommers.com**). I've been booking most of my personal travel online for several years now; it's the only way to go, in my opinion!

- **Shopping.** The number of stores operating on the Internet has now reached tens of thousands. Virtually every big retailer and many small retailers offer the capability to shop and purchase merchandise right from your Web browser. The Internet Mall site collects the Web addresses of more than 22,000 online merchants. Once you enter an online merchant's site, it's just like shopping from a catalog—except it's interactive! (Just make sure you have your credit card handy when you start your online shopping spree.)

I do a lot of shopping online; two of my favorite merchants are Amazon.com (**http://www.amazon.com**) for books and CDnow! (**http://www.cdnow.com/**) for compact discs.

- **Playing Games.** If you like to play computer games, you've probably wondered how you could arrange for head-to-head competition with other gamers. Well, thanks to some innovative gaming sites on the Internet, you can now engage in multi-player PC gaming with other gamers anywhere in the world, linked by the global Internet. While these "multi-player" gaming sites often charge a fee, there are numerous free sites where you can find general gaming information, news, and tips, as well as download the hottest shareware PC games. Look for Happy Puppy (**http://www.happypuppy.com**), Kali (**http://www.kali.net**), and—if you're into video games—VideoGameSpot (**http://www.videogamespot.com**).

- **Creating Your Own Personal Start Page.** Why settle for someone else's idea of a start page when you can design your own? Many sites now offer the capability to customize your own personal start page. You can choose which types of news you want to read, which sports scores and stock quotes you want to track, and which locations you want weather reports for. With a personal start page, you get the news *your* way every time you launch your Web browser.

  I happen to like the custom My Yahoo! page offered by the Yahoo! site (described in Task 50). But the custom pages offered by The Microsoft Network (**http://www.msn.com**) and Infoseek (**http://personal.infoseek.com**) are also nice.

- **Receiving Information on Your Desktop.** If browsing to a custom news page is good, wouldn't it be even better if that custom news were delivered right to your desktop? Thanks to emerging technologies with names like "push content" and "active desktop," you can now receive custom news reports over the Internet, delivered automatically to your own PC.

And, with programs like PointCast, you can display this customized news as a screen saver when you're not using your PC!

- **Creating Your Own Web Page.** By now you've seen enough Web pages that you're probably wondering how easy it would be to create a Web page of your own. Well, the newest generation of Web page editors (typified by Netscape Composer and Microsoft FrontPage) make creating a Web page just about as easy as desktop publishing a paper in Microsoft Word. I'll show you how to create your own personal Web page in just 15 easy steps—after all, this is an *easy* book! Note that there are also specialized services on the Web that exist just to store personal Web pages, such as GeoCities (**http://www. geocities.com**). If, however, you're more interested in looking for other users' personal pages than creating your own, check out the Personal Seek search engine (**http://www.personalseek.com**), created just for searching personal Web pages.

These are just six things you can do on the Web. In reality, you can do a lot more, but there's only room for so much information in this book. I'll leave it to you to discover other Web wonders on your own!

Missing Link

Because the Internet is an ever-changing medium, some of the Web sites and software you see in this book may differ from what you see on the Internet.

Making Travel Plans on the Web

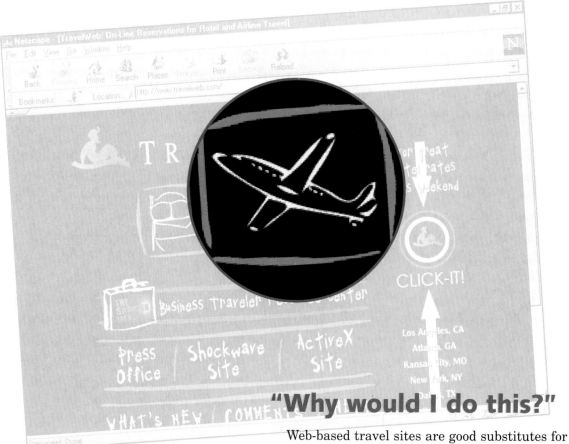

"Why would I do this?"

Web-based travel sites are good substitutes for travel agents. From the comfort of your own keyboard, you can check flight and hotel availability and even book your own reservations. TravelWeb is an all-in-one Web site that makes booking your reservations as easy as a few mouse clicks!

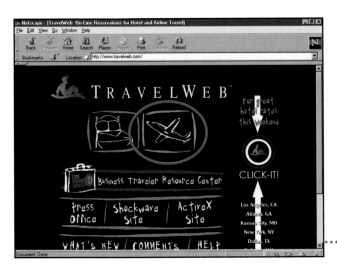

1 Go to the home page of TravelWeb at the following address: **http://www.travelweb.com**. To make airline reservations, click the airplane icon; when the Flight Reservations screen appears, click **Flight Search**.

2 When the Flight Search screen appears, select either **Round Trip** or **One Way**. Select your preferred airline, or choose **No Preference** to see all available flights. Then select your desired departure and return date and time and enter your departure and arrival cities. When you finish, click **Check Flight Availability**.

Puzzled?

If there is more than one airport in a selected city, you'll be prompted to choose the airport from a list of possibilities.

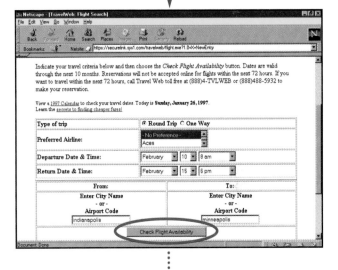

3 TravelWeb displays a list of departing and returning flights. Click the box next to the flights you want to take, and then click **Check Lowest Fare.**

Missing Link

If a flight has a stopover, both segments of the flight are shown.

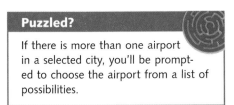

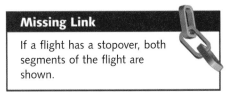

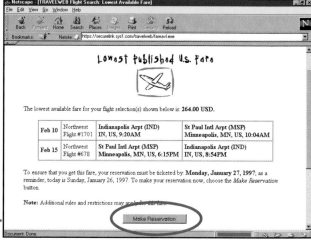

4 The details of your flight appear, along with the lowest available price. If this is acceptable to you, click **Make Reservation**.

5 Enter your traveler and billing information, along with where you want the tickets delivered. Click **Continue Reservation** to see a Verified Reservation form and complete your reservations. Your tickets will be mailed directly to your address.

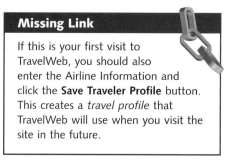

Missing Link

If this is your first visit to TravelWeb, you should also enter the Airline Information and click the **Save Traveler Profile** button. This creates a *travel profile* that TravelWeb will use when you visit the site in the future.

6 To make a hotel reservation, click the bed icon on TravelWeb's home page. When the Hotel Reservations page appears, click **Search the Hotel Database**.

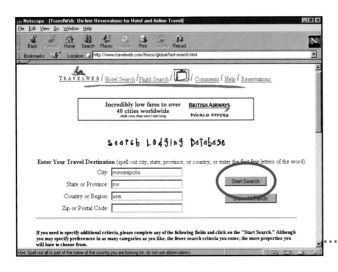

7 Enter the city you want to visit and click **Start Search**. When the list of hotels appears, click an entry to see more information.

8 After you read the information provided, if you want to make a reservation, click **Reservations**. When the Reservations screen appears, click **Check Availability.**

9 Enter your arrival and departure dates, as well as any other preferences. Then click **Send Form**. You'll be presented with a list of available room types and their rates. Click a room/rate type to proceed to the Reservation Request page, where you enter your personal information and credit card number and finalize your reservation. ■

Shopping on the Web

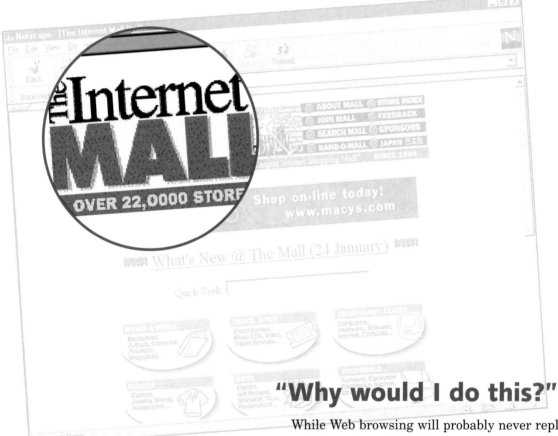

"Why would I do this?"

While Web browsing will probably never replace mall browsing, it's quite convenient to shop for and order merchandise right from your computer keyboard. In fact, shopping via the Internet is a lot like shopping from a direct mail catalog; the only difference is, you don't have to bother making a phone call and dealing with an operator! With so many merchants opening up online storefronts, you want to start at a site that lists just about every store available online. That site is called the Internet Mall.

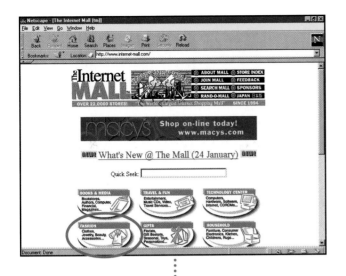

1 Go to the home page of the Internet Mall at the following address: **http://www. internet-mall.com**. Select the type of shopping you want to do, such as **Fashion**.

Missing Link

You can also search for merchants of a particular type by using the Quick Seek function on the home page, or you can view an alphabetical list of merchants by clicking **Store Index**.

2 When the list of types of retailers appears, click a particular type, such as **Clothes**.

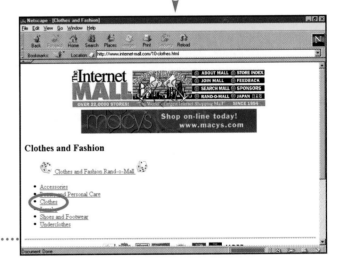

3 From the next list, select the address for the retailer you want to visit. For this example, let's go to the Lands End store. To get there, scroll to the bottom of the screen and click **More Clothes Listings**. (Because there are so many online clothes retailers, you'll have to click through several pages to get to the Ls.) Find the Lands End listing and click its address to go to the Lands End Web site.

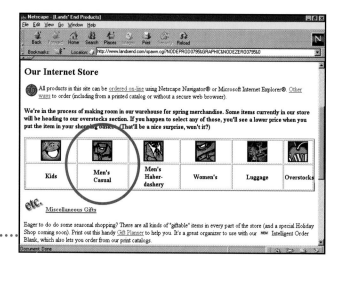

4 When the main Lands End page appears, click **Internet Store** to enter the online store. Like many other online stores, Lands End divides their selections into categories. From the category list, click the category in which you want to shop, such as **Men's Casual**.

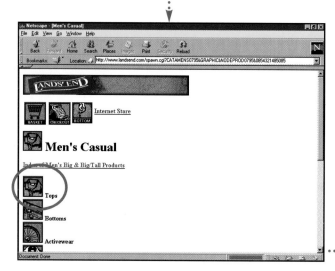

5 An index of products in the Men's Casual category appears. Click the type of product you're interested in, such as **Tops**.

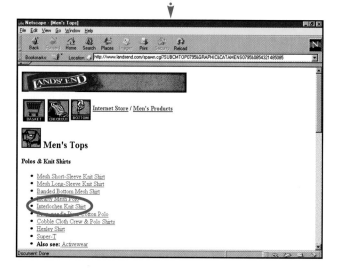

6 Your Web browser displays a list of individual products in the line you selected. Click the product you want to examine, such as **Interlochen Knit Shirt**.

7 You'll see a full description and picture of the selected product. To initiate a purchase, scroll down the page and click the **Buy** icon next to the type of shirt you want.

8 To complete your order, fill in the size, color, and other specific information on the selected product. When you finish, click **Place Item in Basket**.

Missing Link

Many Web sites use what is called a *secure server* to provide secure credit transactions—in which it's unlikely that your credit card information will be intercepted and stolen online. (If your browser doesn't support secure transactions, you'll receive a message to that effect, and you may need to phone in your order.)

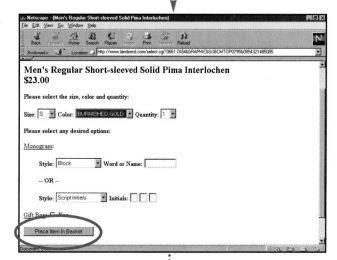

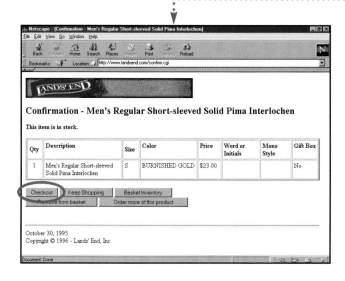

9 Next, you'll see a confirmation page. To finalize your order, click the **Checkout** button. When you're prompted to fill in the ordering information, enter your name, address, phone number, and (on the following page) your credit card number and expiration date. Lands End will finalize your order, and you should expect your new shirt sometime in the next few days! ■

Playing Games on the Web

"Why would I do this?"

Many new PC games offer a multi-player mode. Thanks to several multi-player game-related sites on the Web, such as the Total Entertainment Network, you can take advantage of this multi-player mode and play Duke Nukem, Quake, and other games over the Internet with players from all around the world. Most of these sites use their own software (instead of a normal Web browser), so the first step is downloading the game-playing software. After you install the software, dial up your Internet provider, start the multi-player software, and start gaming!

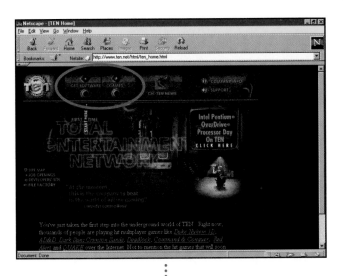

1 Go to the Total Entertainment Network's main page at the following address: **http://www.ten.net**. To download the TEN software, click **Get Software** and follow the on-screen instructions. To download shareware versions of specific games, click **Games** and follow the on-screen instructions.

Puzzled?

To use the TEN software, you need a connection through an Internet service provider.

2 When you launch the TEN software, enter your name and password, and then click **Connect**. The TEN software automatically connects you to TEN's site.

Missing Link

To access the Total Entertainment Network, you must first subscribe to the TEN service. There are two subscription plans: Hourly ($9.95/month with five free hours; $1.95 for each additional hour) and Flat-Rate ($29.95/month; no hourly fees).

3 To play a game online, select the game from the Games list and click **Play**.

Missing Link

You must have a copy of the game installed on your computer to play it over TEN.

4 TEN divides up its many games into what it calls *zones* and *arenas*. Select a zone and an arena, and then click **Go**.

Missing Link

TEN ranks its zones and arenas in increasing order of difficulty. It will warn you if you choose an arena that is not recommended for your specific skill level.

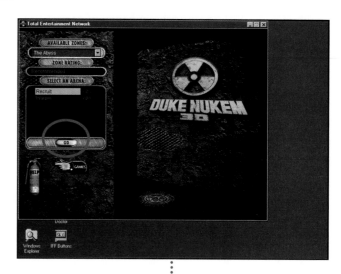

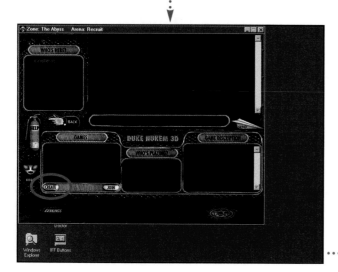

5 The main game window appears. To join an existing game, highlight the game and click **Join**. To create a new game, click **Create**.

6 To create a new game, give it a name and a description, and then click **OK**. A DOS window opens, and you wait for other players to join your game. Once the game starts, you're on your own!

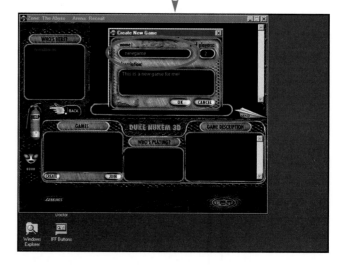

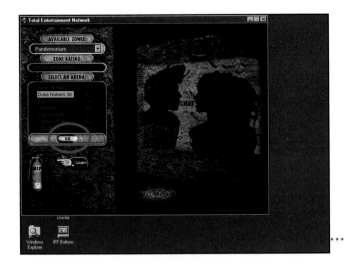

7 To chat with other users, return to TEN's main screen and click **Chat**. You'll be prompted to choose an arena (a chat area). Do so, and then click **Go**.

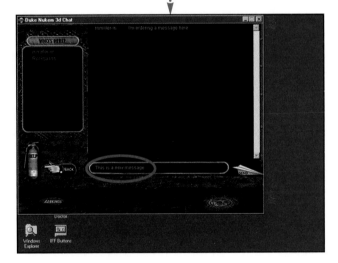

8 Messages from other users appear in the top pane. Enter your messages in the bottom box and click **Send**. ■

Creating Your Own Personal Start Page

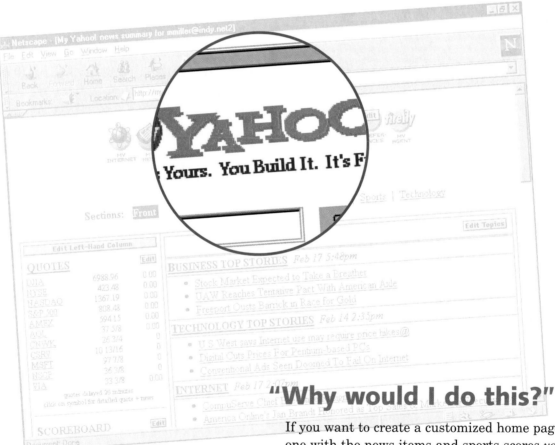

"Why would I do this?"

If you want to create a customized home page—one with the news items and sports scores *you* want to read—the place to start is at Yahoo! You see, in addition to being the leading search site, Yahoo! also offers a special customized start page service called My Yahoo! You can customize My Yahoo! in dozens of different ways, creating your perfect personalized start page.

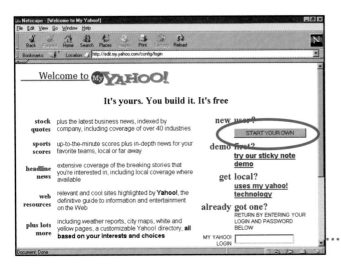

1 Go to the main My Yahoo! page at the following address:

http://my.yahoo.com

Click the **Start Your Own** button to begin.

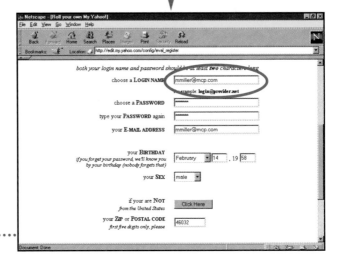

2 Create a Login Name (your e-mail address is good) and a Password. Then enter your e-mail address, birthday, sex, ZIP code, and occupation. Click **Register Me Now!** to proceed.

3 When the list of topics appears, click the boxes next to those of interest to you.

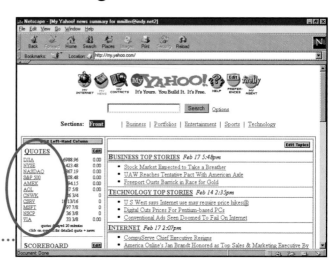

4 Scroll down the page to the Stock Quotes section and enter the ticker symbols of any stocks you'd like to track. Separate the stocks you list with either a space or a comma. Click **Use These Interests** when you're ready to proceed.

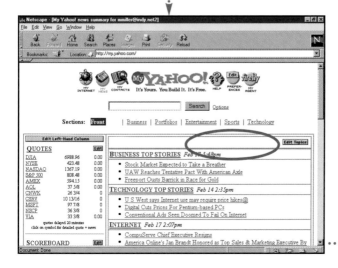

5 When the confirmation page appears, click **Take Me to My Yahoo!** This displays your new personalized page.

Missing Link

You can alter your preferences at any time by clicking the **Edit** button next to any section on the My Yahoo! page. If you want to change your password or ZIP code, click **Edit Preferences** at the *top* of the My Yahoo! page.

6 You're not done yet. Your "personal" page contains some default settings that you'll probably want to change. For example, to edit the sports scores you want to see, click the **Edit** button next to Scoreboard.

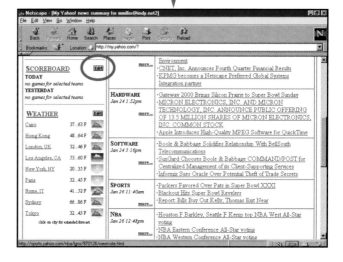

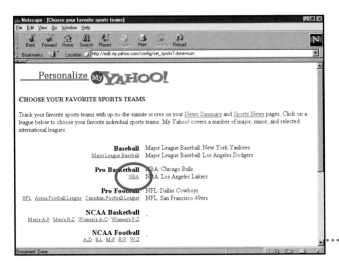

7 When the next screen appears, click the sports you want to track, and then select the individual teams within those sports. When you finish, click **Done**.

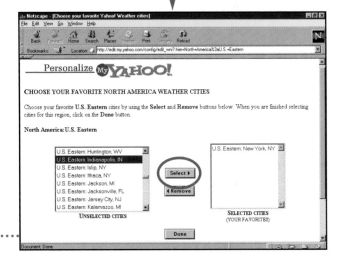

8 To select which cities you want displayed in your weather list, click the **Edit** button next to Weather. Over the next two pages, select the areas and cities you want to track. When you finish, click **Done**.

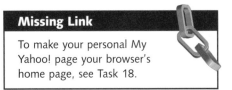

9 Yahoo! has also personalized a list of Web sites that correspond to your selected interests. Click **My Internet** to see that list. ■

Missing Link

To make your personal My Yahoo! page your browser's home page, see Task 18.

163

TASK

51

Receiving Information on Your Desktop

"Why would I do this?"

The Internet is a great medium for "narrowcasting" news and other information. Companies can use the Internet to deliver personalized news and other information direct to your desktop, without any effort on your part. One of the first—and most popular—of these narrowcasting services is the PointCast Network. PointCast works in the background on your PC, retrieving news and other information and displaying it either on-demand or as your PC's screen saver.

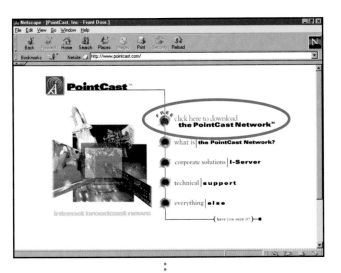

1 To obtain a free copy of the PointCast software, go to PointCast's home page at **http://www.pointcast.com**. Click where it says **Click Here to Download**, and then follow the instructions to download the software.

Missing Link

PointCast only works with personal computers; you can't use PointCast with a WebTV box.

2 After you install the PointCast software, you need to configure it for your needs. Launch the software and click the **Options** button.

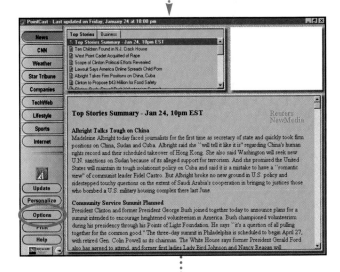

Missing Link

If you have a dedicated Internet connection through your network at work, you can choose to have PointCast update automatically. If you do, you'll always have the latest news, without having to click the Update button.

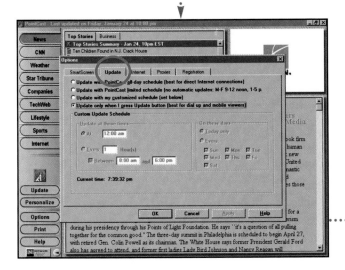

3 From the Options dialog box, click the **Update** tab and select the method you want to use to update your PointCast information. If you're connecting to the Internet via a phone line, select **Update Only When I Press Update Button**, and then click **OK**.

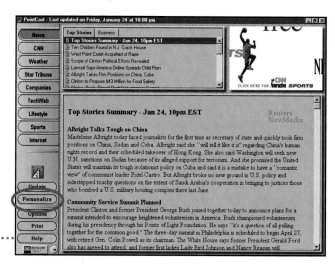

4 To select what news and information you receive, click the **Personalize** button.

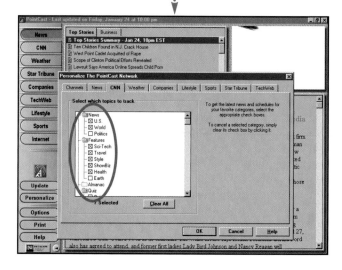

5 Click the **Channels** tab to select the news/information "channels" you want to receive. Use the **Move Up** and **Move Down** buttons to place them in the order you want them.

6 Use the specific channel tabs to select options for each individual news/information channel. When you finish, click **OK**.

7 To read the news in a given channel, click the desired channel button, select the desired topic tab, and then click the story you want to read. The text of the story appears in the bottom pane.

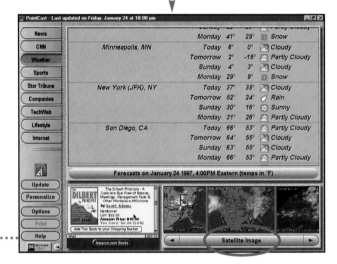

8 Click the **Weather** button, and you see scrolling forecasts for selected cities in the top pane, as well as selected weather maps in the bottom pane. To see a larger view of the weather maps, click the **Satellite Image** button.

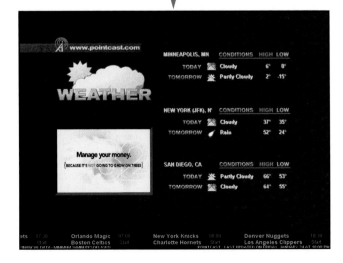

9 PointCast automatically installs itself as your PC's screen saver. After a specified period of inactivity, your screen will blank, and PointCast will show news and other information in a lively full-screen display. ∎

TASK 52

Creating Your Own Web Page

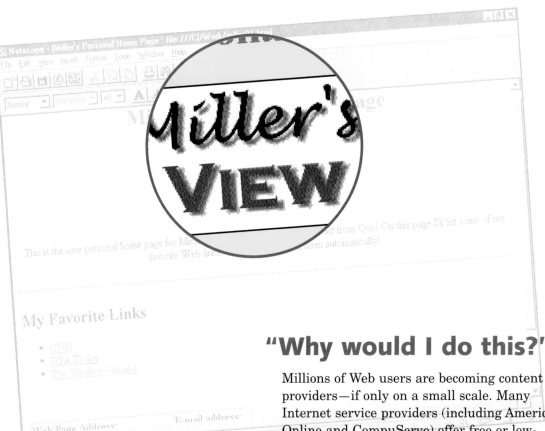

"Why would I do this?"

Millions of Web users are becoming content providers—if only on a small scale. Many Internet service providers (including America Online and CompuServe) offer free or low-charge storage for users' personal Web pages. And with the advent of Netscape Composer and Microsoft FrontPage, creating a Web page is as easy as typing and clicking. There's no messy HTML code to learn. Because Composer is included as part of the Netscape Communicator suite, I'll use it to show you how to create a "quick and dirty" personal Web page.

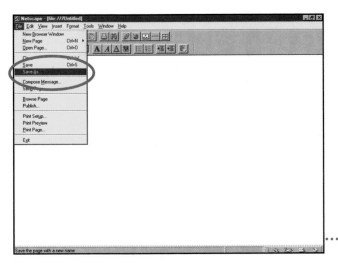

1 When you launch Netscape Composer, a new blank Web page is created. Pull down the **File** menu and select **Save As** to save this file with a name of your choice. Composer automatically assigns the file an HTM extension.

2 To give your file a name that users on the Internet will see, pull down the **Format** menu and select **Page Title**. When the Page Properties dialog box appears, select the **General** tab, enter the name of the page in the **Title** text box, enter your name in the **Author** text box, and type a brief description in the **Description** text box. *Don't* click OK when you're done; there's more to do in this dialog box!

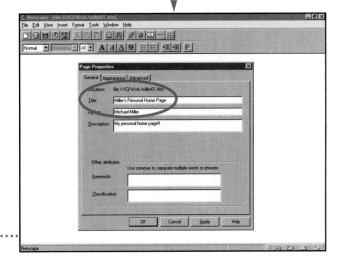

3 In the Page Properties dialog box, click the **Appearance** tab and click **Use Custom Colors**. Select a scheme from the **Color Schemes** pull-down menu or click the **Background** button and select a color from the Color chooser. (If you select a dark background, you'll need to choose a light text color.) Click **OK**.

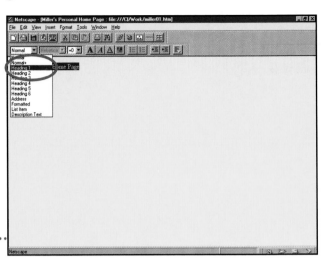

4 Start your Web page with a big title. Enter your title text in the edit window, and then pull down the **Paragraph** style list and select **Heading 1**.

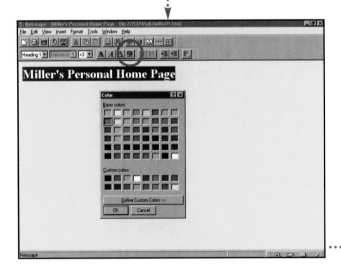

5 Now add some color to your title by highlighting the text, clicking the **Font Color** button, and selecting a color from the Color chooser.

6 Center the title text by highlighting the text, clicking the **Alignment** button, and selecting the centered text button.

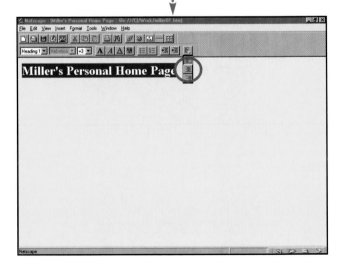

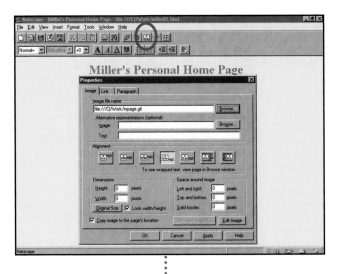

7 To add a picture to your page, move your cursor to the end of the title text and press **Enter** to start a new line. (That line should be centered, just like the title text.) Click the **Insert Image** button, and when the Properties dialog box appears, click the **Image** tab. Enter the file name of the graphics file you want to insert in the **Image File Name** box and click **OK**.

8 Move your cursor to the end of the second line (to the right of the graphic) and press **Enter** to start another new line. Add some descriptive text. The text will automatically wrap, so you don't have to press Enter at the end of each line. (Notice that the Paragraph style for this text is Normal, which is what it should be.) When you finish entering text, press **Enter** to start a new blank line.

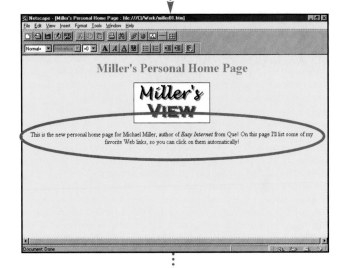

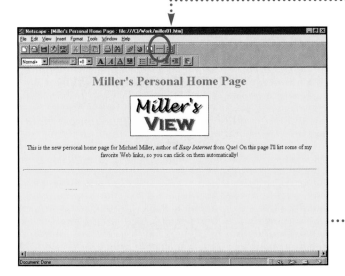

9 Add a horizontal line under this text by clicking the **Insert Horz. Line** button.

10 Add a subhead by typing new text, highlighting it, pulling down the **Paragraph** style list, and selecting **Heading 2**. Left-align this text by highlighting it, clicking the **Alignment** button, and choosing the left alignment button.

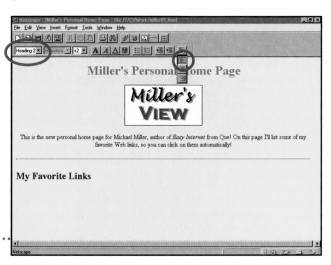

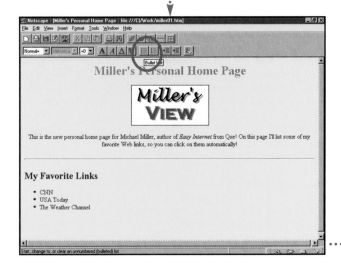

11 Begin a bulleted list by clicking the **Bullet List** button. Enter the text for the list. Then end the bulleted list by positioning the cursor on the line *after* the list and clicking the **Bullet List** button.

12 To add a link to another Web page, highlight the text that will be linked and click the **Make Link** button. When the Properties dialog box appears, select the **Link** tab and enter the Web address (URL) of the page you're linking to in the **Link to a Page Location** box. When you finish, click **OK**.

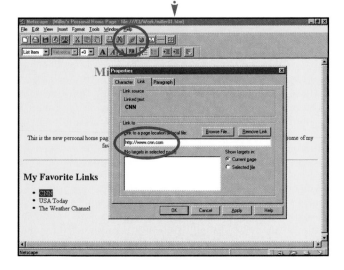

Missing Link

Hypertext links allow you to link to additional information without having to include that information directly on your page.

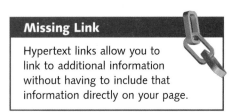

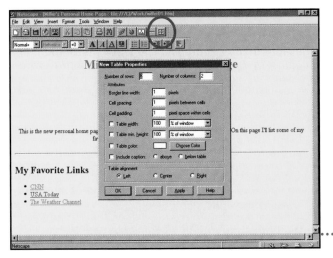

13 Some information is best displayed in tabular format. Add a table at the current cursor position by clicking the **Table** button. When the New Table Properties dialog box appears, select the number of rows and columns for your table, change any other properties you want, and click **OK**. When you enter text in the table, it will automatically size itself to fit the text.

14 Add your e-mail address at the bottom of the page and create a "mail to" link that automatically sends mail to your address. To do so, highlight your address and click the **Make Link** button. When the Properties dialog box appears, select the **Link** tab and enter **mailto:_XXX@XXX_**, where _XXX@XXX_ is your e-mail address. Then click **OK**.

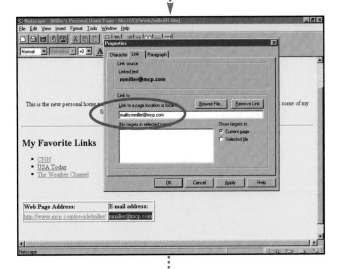

Missing Link

When a user clicks a "mail to" link, his browser opens an e-mail program with a pre-addressed message that's ready to be sent.

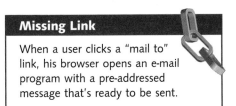

15 Save your page by clicking the **Save** button. To see your page in a Web browser, click the **View in Browser** button. This launches Netscape Navigator and loads your page. ■

Missing Link

To post your Web page to a Web server, you'll need to contact your ISP or online service to see how much they charge for storing personal Web pages (many ISPs do this for free) and for information on how to upload your pages to their site.

PART IX

Six Things to Know About E-Mail

ELECTRONIC MAIL IS A LOT DIFFERENT from the mail delivered by the United States Postal Service. In fact, veteran Internetters often refer to normal mail as "snail mail" because it's so much slower than e-mail.

When you send an electronic "letter" to another Internet user, that letter travels from your computer to your Internet service provider, to the Internet, to your recipient's Internet service provider, to your recipient's personal computer, and to your recipient—almost *instantly*. Your

messages travel at the speed of electrons over a number of phone lines and Internet connections, automatically routed to the right place just about as fast as you can click the "send" button.

That's a *lot* different from using the U.S. Postal Service.

How does your message know where it's supposed to go? What keeps your message from taking a wrong turn at Albuquerque and ending up halfway around the world from where you wanted it to go?

Well, it all has to do with *addresses*. That's right, you put an address on your Internet e-mail, pretty much the same way you put an address on an envelope. And every Internet user has his or her own unique address, so that e-mail can be routed directly to the intended recipient.

An Internet address is composed of three parts:

- The user's **log-in name**
- The @ sign
- The user's **domain** (usually the Internet name of their service provider)

Let's say you're sending an e-mail message to your friend George Jetson, and his log-in name is **gjetson**. He has an e-mail account with a service provider called SpacelyNet, which has a domain name of **spacely.com**. You would address your message like this:

gjetson@spacely.com

It's that simple.

Another neat thing about e-mail on the Internet is the existence of thousands of special-interest *mailing lists*. These lists are run by *list managers,* who encourage discussion and debate on selected topics by multiple users. If you're interested in Marilyn Monroe, for example, you can subscribe to the Marilyn Monroe mailing list. From time to time, you'll receive (via e-mail) a batch of messages from other mailing list members interested in Marilyn Monroe; you can also send mail to other members of the group. (To subscribe to this particular list, follow the steps in Task 58 and send your subscription to **marilyn-request@mozart.lib.uchicago.edu**.)

To send and receive e-mail, you use an e-mail program. Lots of e-mail programs are available; for the examples in this book, we'll use Netscape Messenger, which is included with the Netscape Communicator suite.

By the way, if you'd like to send e-mail to me, my official Que e-mail address is: **mmiller@mcp.com**.

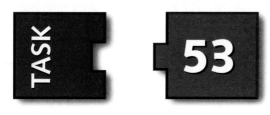

Retrieving and Reading E-Mail Messages

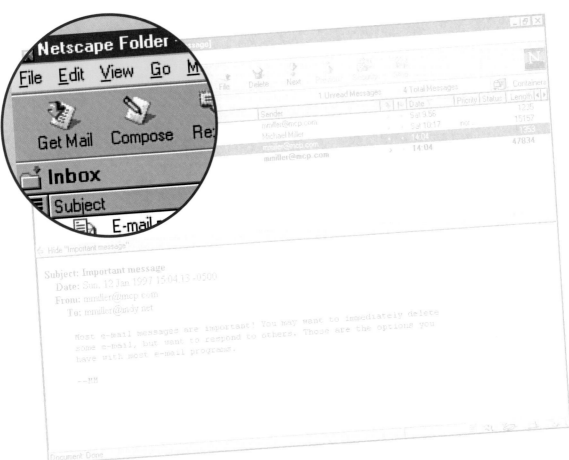

"Why would I do this?"

Your e-mail program automatically checks to see if you've received any new e-mail messages when it first starts up, and then again every so many minutes afterwards. In this task you learn how to retrieve e-mail from your "inbox" for your reading pleasure.

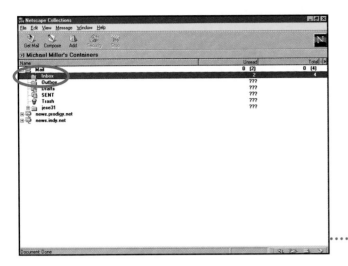

1 Launch your e-mail program. Any waiting e-mail messages are stored in the "inbox." Double-click the **Inbox** icon, and your inbox opens, listing any waiting e-mail messages. (If no messages are listed, you have no waiting mail.)

2 Some programs, like Netscape Messenger, show the contents of the selected message in a separate pane. Other programs require you to double-click a message to read it. If necessary, double-click a message.

Missing Link

With most e-mail programs, you can also get your e-mail manually by clicking the **Get Mail** button.

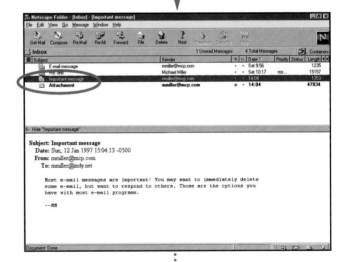

3 When you double-click the selected message, a new window opens, displaying the message's contents. ■

Missing Link

When you finish reading the message, you can either reply to it (see Task 54), file a copy to your hard disk (by clicking the **File** button), or delete it (by clicking the **Delete** button).

177

Responding to E-Mail Messages

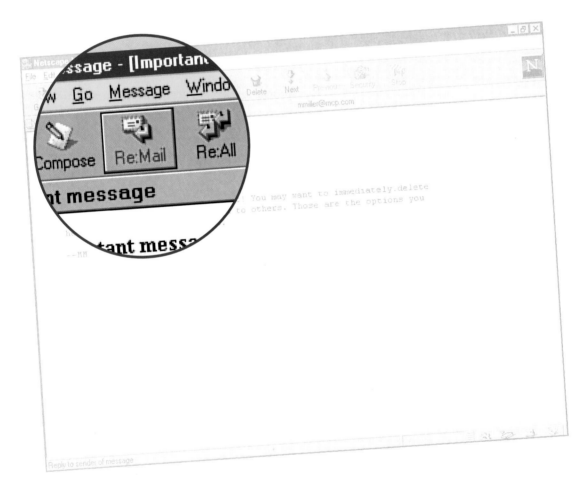

"Why would I do this?"

Many times you will want to send a reply to an e-mail message. In this task, you'll learn how to compose a reply and to automatically send the reply to the sender of the original message.

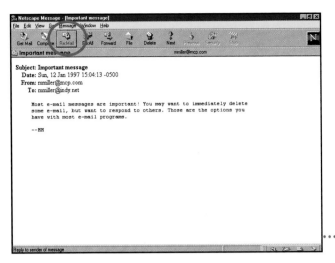

1 To reply to a message, click the **Re:Mail** button.

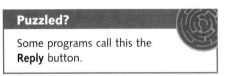

Puzzled?

Some programs call this the **Reply** button.

2 A new window opens. This window shows the sender of the previous message as the new recipient, and it references ("re:") the subject of the previous message.

Missing Link

It is good e-mail etiquette to "quote" the original text in your reply. Just place the cursor where you want to insert the quoted text and click the **Quote Original** button.

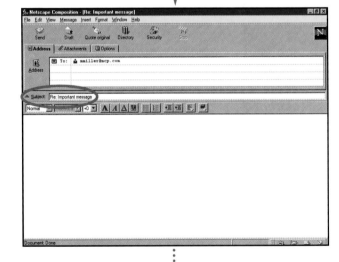

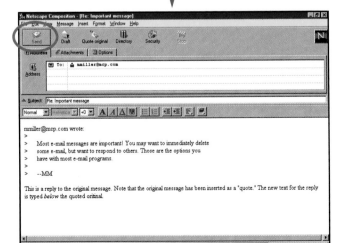

3 You can now enter new text into this e-mail message. When you finish typing, click the **Send** button to send the message on its way. ■

TASK **55**

Creating a New E-Mail Message

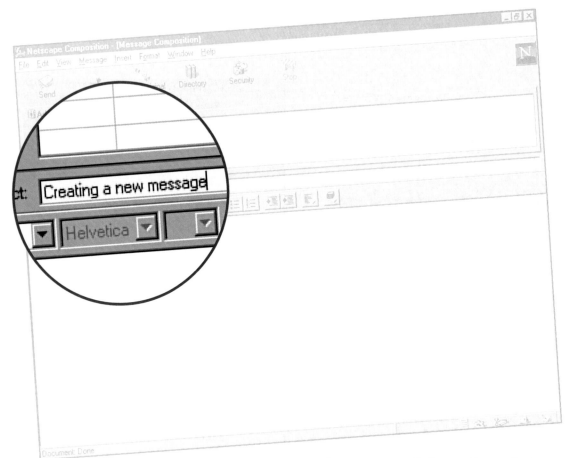

"Why would I do this?"

One of the most useful things about the Internet is the capability to send electronic mail to other users. In this task, you learn how to create a new e-mail message and then send that message to another user.

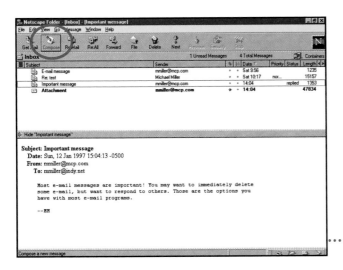

1 Click the **Compose** button to open a new message window.

2 Move the cursor to the Address box, click on the first blank line, and enter the e-mail address of your recipient. Press the **Tab** key to move to the **Subject** box, and then enter the subject of your message.

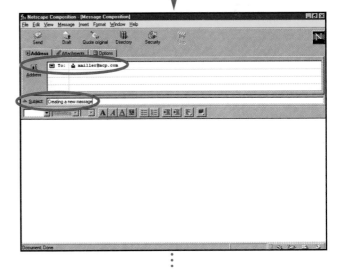

Missing Link

You can enter multiple recipients, as well as recipients who are to receive a "carbon copy" (cc) of your message. You can even send some recipients a "blind" carbon copy (bcc) so that no other recipients can see that the bcc'd recipient actually received a copy.

3 Press the **Tab** key again to move down to the body of the message, and then begin typing your message. When you finish typing, click the **Send** button to send it on its way. ■

Missing Link

Some e-mail programs let you attach other files that will "ride" along with your e-mail message. In Netscape Messenger, select the **Attachments** tab, click the **Attach File** button, and select the file you want to attach.

181

56

Searching for E-Mail Addresses

"Why would I do this?"

Millions of people have access to the Internet— maybe some of your old friends are even online! When you want to search for an e-mail address, go to a dedicated e-mail search engine on the World Wide Web, such as Bigfoot.

No single directory lists every possible e-mail address, so if you can't find the person you're looking for at Bigfoot, try another directory, such as WhoWhere (**http://www. whowhere.com**). You should also check out **http://sunsite.unc.edu/ ~masha/** for more tips on how to find e-mail addresses.

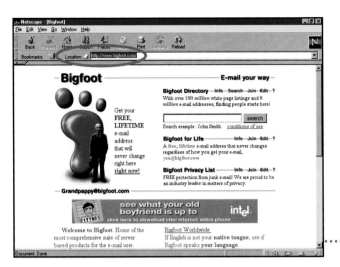

1 Use your Web browser to go to Bigfoot's main page at the following address:

http://www.bigfoot.com

2 Enter the first and last name of the person for whom you're searching in the search box. Then click the **Search** button.

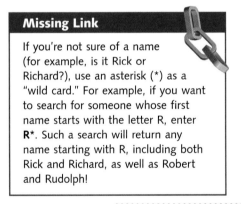

Missing Link

If you're not sure of a name (for example, is it Rick or Richard?), use an asterisk (*) as a "wild card." For example, if you want to search for someone whose first name starts with the letter R, enter **R***. Such a search will return any name starting with R, including both Rick and Richard, as well as Robert and Rudolph!

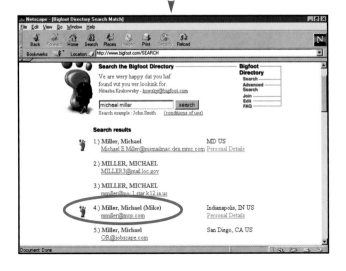

3 Bigfoot returns a list of e-mail addresses that match your request. If you find the name you're looking for, you can click the e-mail address to automatically send an e-mail to that person. ■

Obtaining a List of Mailing Lists

"Why would I do this?"

Internet mailing lists are like special interest discussion groups. When you subscribe to a list, you receive periodic mailings (via e-mail) that contain messages to and from other members. (Mailing lists are a lot like UseNet newsgroups—discussed in Part 10—except they use e-mail as the discussion medium.) Before you can subscribe, however, you need to know a little bit about the list. And it also helps to look at a list of all the lists available!

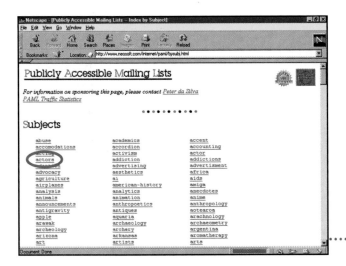

1 To view a list of mailing lists sorted by subject, use your Web browser to go to the Publicly Accessible Mailing Lists page, located at the following address:

http://www.neosoft.com/internet/paml/bysubj.html

Then click the subject you're interested in.

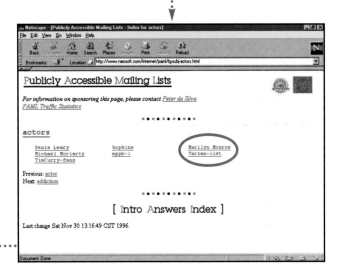

2 When the list of lists within that topic appears, click the name of the mailing list you're most interested in.

3 Details about this particular mailing list appear, including instructions on how to subscribe. ■

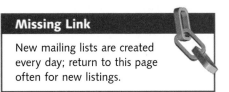

Missing Link

New mailing lists are created every day; return to this page often for new listings.

185

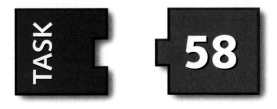

Subscribing to an E-Mail Mailing List

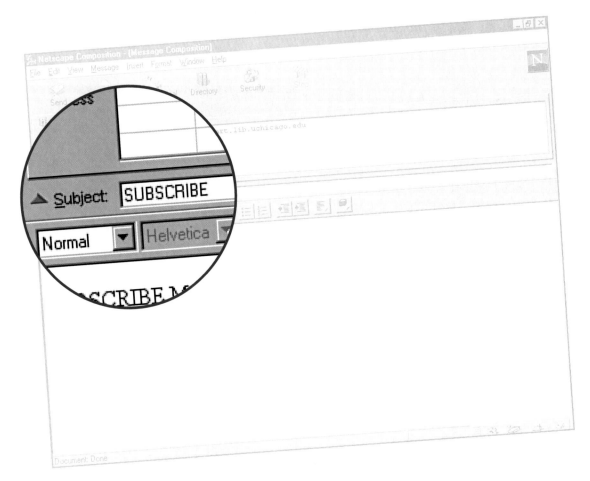

"Why would I do this?"

To subscribe to an e-mail mailing list, you must send e-mail to the list manager noting that you want to become a member. You have to follow a particular format in your message, however.

In this task you learn how to subscribe to a mailing list. After you do so, you should begin receiving mail from the list within two or three days.

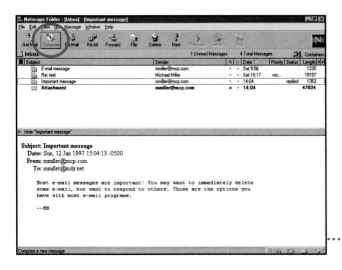

1 Click the **Compose** button to open a new message window.

Puzzled?

Sometimes a mailing list has one address for subscribing and a different address for normal posting. Try not to get the addresses confused!

2 Click on the first blank line in the Address box and enter the e-mail address of the mailing list. Press the **Tab** key to move to the **Subject** box, and then enter **SUBSCRIBE** as the subject of your message.

Missing Link

Some lists send out messages from other members either individually or in digest version. (A *digest* is a compilation of multiple messages, generally sent once a day or once a month.) In this example, you use a different address to subscribe to the digest version: **marilyn-d-request@mozart.lib.uchicago.edu**.

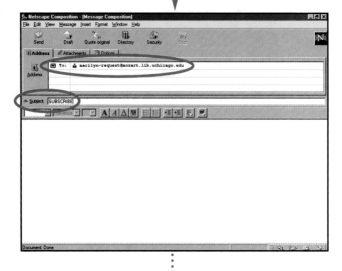

3 Press **Tab** again. Then enter **SUBSCRIBE** *listname firstname lastname*, where *listname* is the name of the mailing list, and *firstname* and *lastname* are your first and last names. Click **Send**, and you should begin receiving mail in days. ■

Missing Link

To cancel a mailing subscription, send a message to the list with **UNSUBSCRIBE** as the subject and **UNSUBSCRIBE** *listname* as the message.

PART X

Five Things to Know About UseNet Newsgroups

USENET IS A NETWORK that operates within the overall confines of the Internet. Its purpose is to broadcast messages to and from users with similar interests, using special interest forums called *newsgroups*.

A newsgroup is an electronic gathering place for people with similar interests. Within a newsgroup users post messages (called *articles*) about a variety of topics; other users read these articles and, when so disposed, respond. The result is a kind of on-going, freeform discussion in which dozens of users may participate.

In many ways, a newsgroup is like an old-fashioned town meeting. Anyone can attend, and anyone can speak his or her mind. At times, things can get a bit disorganized, and it's not uncommon for several people to talk about different things at the same time. But all in all, a lot of interesting opinions are expressed for all to hear.

Because of this inherently chaotic atmosphere, newsgroup articles tend to be grouped in *threads*. A thread is simply a single message topic and all the related articles responding to either the original posting or subsequent responses. A lot of users prefer to read their newsgroup articles in threads so they can follow the drift of a particular discussion without being interrupted by dozens of other discussions.

You may wonder what makes a newsgroup different from an e-mail mailing list. Well, they are pretty similar in that they both serve as gathering places for people with similar interests. The main difference is that mailing lists tend to be a little more organized and focus on more specific topics, while newsgroups are open forums in which anyone can participate. Most mailing lists have fewer members than many newsgroups because mailing lists must be moderated by a single individual. Newsgroups, as you'll soon discover, don't have much moderation at all!

In fact, one of the problems with the public nature of newsgroups is the posting of *commercial* messages—often referred to as *spam*. Because anyone can post, commercial entities pushing their own Web sites, products, or "get rich quick" schemes sometimes clog the message flow in popular newsgroups. Unfortunately, there's no way to avoid this spam—save not reading the messages.

Even though newsgroup discussions tend to get a little chaotic, the groups themselves are part of a fairly rigid organization. UseNet organizes groups according to the categories outlined in the following table.

Of course, these are just the *major* categories. There are dozens of more specialized categories, increasing the total number of newsgroups to more than 15,000!

The name of a newsgroup also follows set conventions. Newsgroup names flow from left to right in order of focus, with levels separated by periods. For example, a newsgroup in the *recreational* section (rec) discussing the *art* of the *cinema* is called the **rec.arts.cinema** group.

You use a *newsreader* software program to subscribe to newsgroups and participate in newsgroup discussions. I've used the Netscape Messenger component of the Netscape Communicator suite for the examples in this section; other newsreader programs work in a similar fashion. Note, however, that at this point in time, WebTV does not offer UseNet access. If you subscribe to America Online or CompuServe, you'll use the built-in newsreaders provided by these services.

Major UseNet Newsgroup Categories

Category	Interests
alt	Alternative topics; generally related to areas that inspire a lot of different opinions (This category has the largest number of newsgroups, covering topics from politics to sex.)
bit	LISTSERV mailing lists from the BITNET network, redistributed in newsgroup format
biz	Business-oriented product announcements
comp	Computer-related topics
k12	Topics related to education in grades kindergarten through 12
misc	Miscellaneous topics
news	Topics related to netnews system administration
rec	Recreational topics
sci	Science topics
soc	Topics related to social issues
talk	Conversational—and controversial—topics

Subscribing to Newsgroups

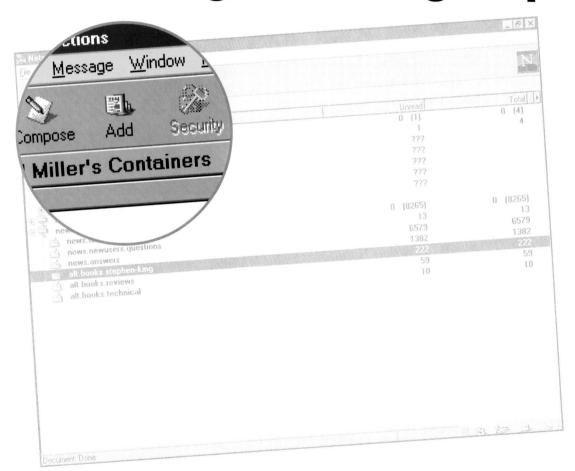

"Why would I do this?"

Before you can read articles in a newsgroup, you first have to *subscribe* to the newsgroup. With more than 15,000 newsgroups available, you need a powerful way to search for the groups you want to subscribe to! This task shows you how to find and subscribe to specific newsgroups.

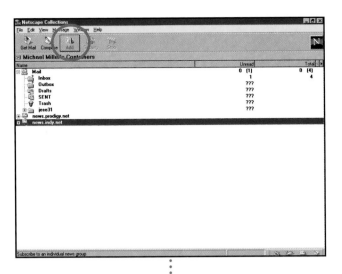

1 From the Netscape Collections window, click the **Add** button.

Missing Link

The first time you run Netscape Messenger, it will take several minutes to load all fifteen thousand newsgroups.

2 There are two ways to add a new newsgroup to your list. The first way is to select the **All Newsgroups** tab, scroll through the list of newsgroups, select the group you want to add, and then click the **Subscribe** button.

Missing Link

Groups within categories are "collapsed" in the directory tree listing. Click the plus sign (**+**) to expand an individual category listing to show all groups, or click the **Expand All** button to expand all category trees.

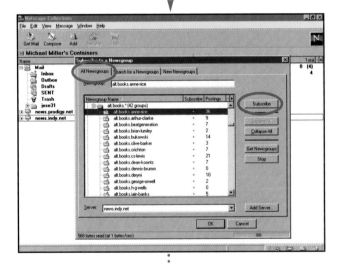

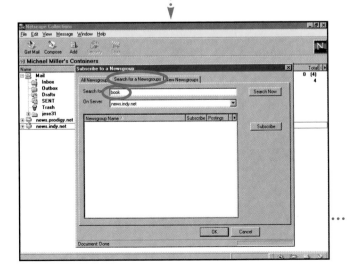

3 The more efficient way to find an individual newsgroup is to select the **Search for a Newsgroup** tab, enter a descriptive phrase in the **Search For:** box, and then click the **Search Now** button.

4 A list of groups containing the specified phrase appears. Select the specific group to which you want to subscribe, and then click the **Subscribe** button.

Missing Link

You can determine the popularity of a newsgroup by looking at the number in the Postings column for that group. A group with lots of postings has more "traffic" than a group with just a few postings.

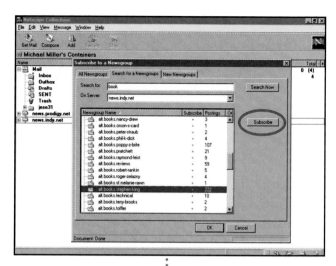

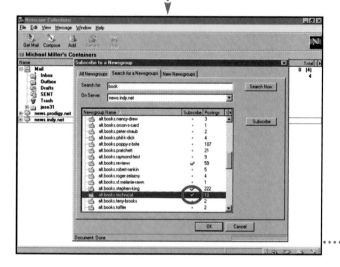

5 When you subscribe to a group, a check mark appears in the Subscribe column of the window. When you finish subscribing to groups, click the **OK** button.

6 The groups you've subscribed to are now listed in the main Netscape Collections window. ■

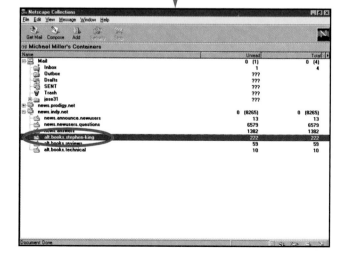

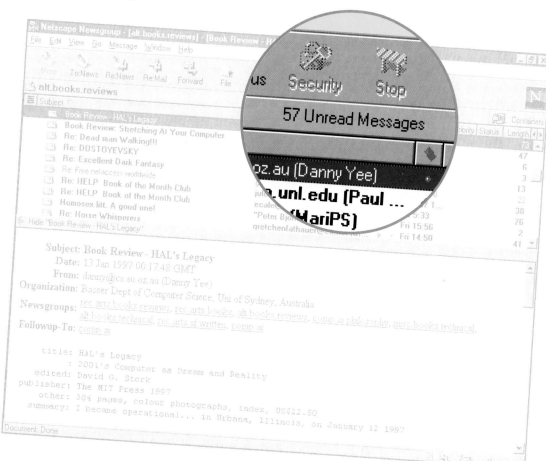

Reading Newsgroup Articles

"Why would I do this?"

The main reason you access a newsgroup is to read articles from other group members. In this task, you'll select a specific newsgroup and follow a thread of articles on a topic you're interested in.

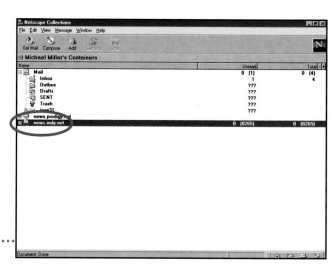

1 In the Netscape Collections window, click the plus sign (+) next to your newsgroup server to show all the groups you've subscribed to.

2 Double-click the newsgroup you want to read.

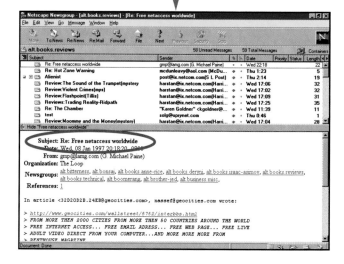

3 The Netscape Newsgroup window opens, with individual articles listed in the top pane and the contents of a selected article in the bottom pane.

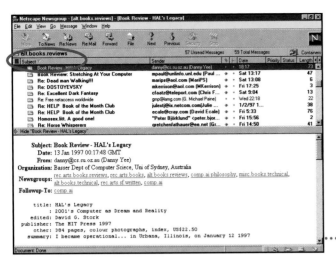

4 To sort articles by subject, click the **Subject** bar above the list of articles.

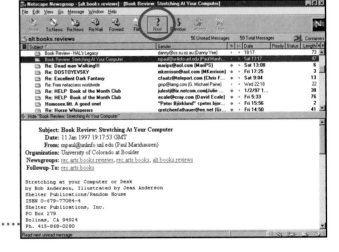

5 To read the next article in the list, click the **Next** button.

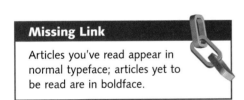

Missing Link

Articles you've read appear in normal typeface; articles yet to be read are in boldface.

6 Return to the newsgroup listing by pulling down the **Window** menu and selecting **Collections**. ■

Responding to and Posting New Newsgroup Articles

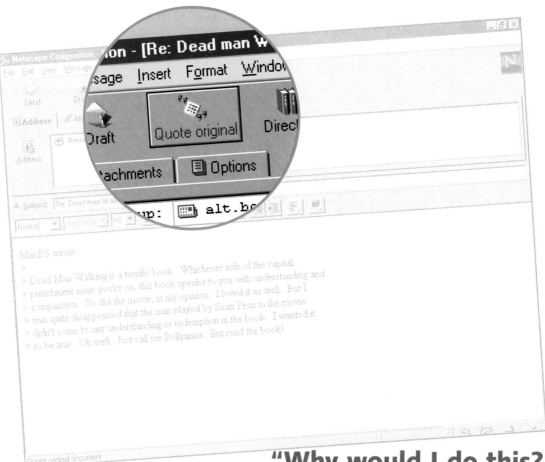

"Why would I do this?"

Reading articles is fun, but a time will come when you'll have an opinion you want to express. To add your opinion to the thread, you'll need to reply to a particular article. Or you can start a new thread by posting a new article. In this task, you learn how to reply to a newsgroup article.

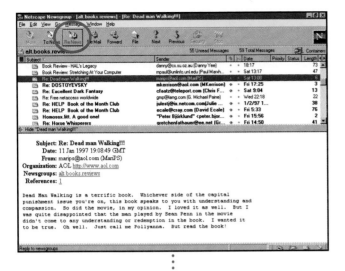

1 With a newsgroup open, select an article to display in the bottom pane. To reply to this article in the newsgroup, click the **Re:News** button.

Missing Link

You can reply privately (via e-mail) to the creator of a message by clicking the **Re:Mail** button.

2 The Netscape Composition window appears, with the address and subject boxes already filled in. Click the **Quote Original** button to insert text from the original message.

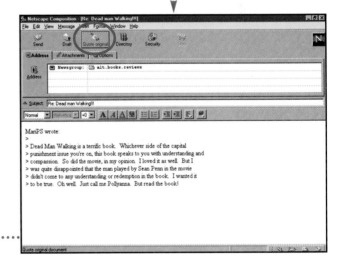

3 Type your message in the large message box below the quoted text. Then click the **Send** button to post your reply to the newsgroup.

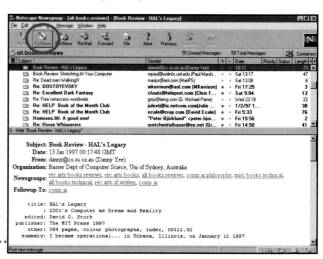

4 To post a new message to a newsgroup, open the newsgroup and click the **To:News** button.

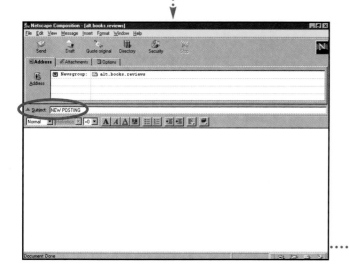

5 When the Netscape Composition window appears, the address (the name of the newsgroup) is automatically filled in. Enter the subject of your article in the **Subject** box, and then press the **Tab** key to move to the large message box.

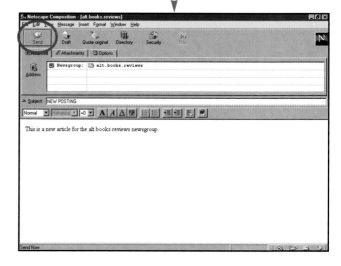

6 Enter your text in the large message box, and then click the **Send** button to post this new message to the newsgroup. ■

Viewing and Saving Picture Files

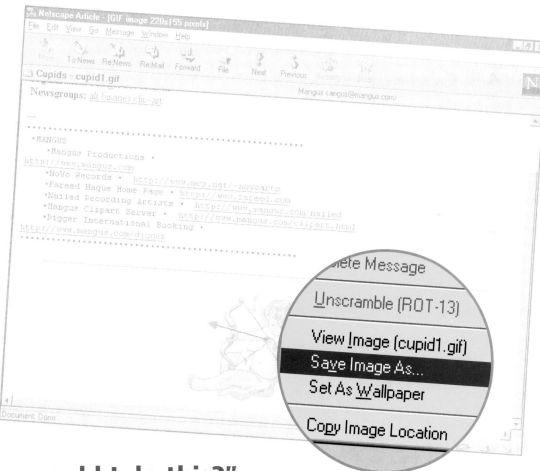

"Why would I do this?"

Many newsgroups exist to distribute files—generally graphics or sound files. These files are stored in *binary* format (so-called because if you looked at the raw coded file, it would look like a series of binary numbers). Most of the newsgroups specializing in these files are in the alt.binaries category. This task shows you how to view picture files and save them to your hard disk.

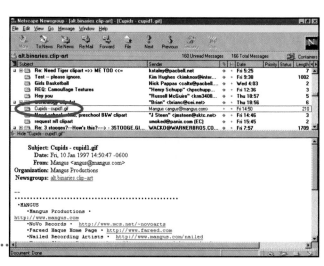

1 Go to a newsgroup that contains postings as binary files, such as **alt.binaries. clipart**. Double-click the article you want to view.

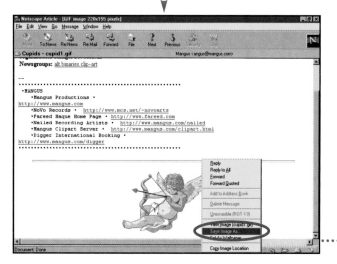

2 An Article window appears, displaying the contents of the binary file (generally a picture). To save the picture to your hard disk, move your cursor over the image, click the *right* mouse button to display the pop-up menu, and then click **Save Image As**.

3 In the Save As dialog box, select a location and enter a name for the file, and then click **Save**. ■

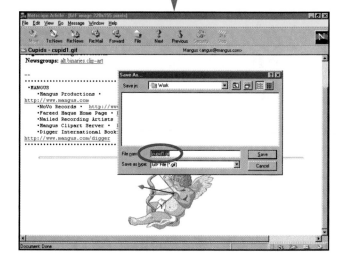

Searching DejaNews for UseNet Articles

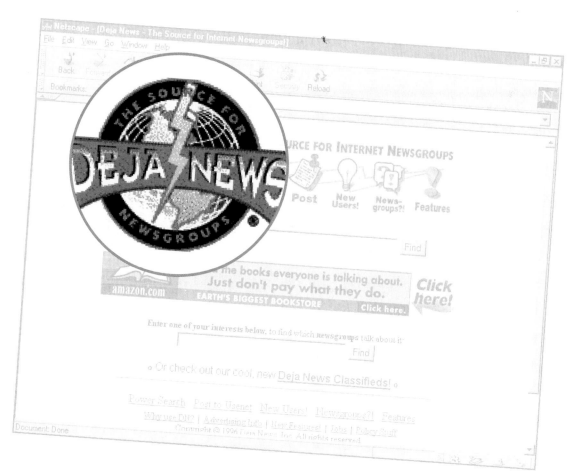

"Why would I do this?"

Articles stay available in a newsgroup for only a limited period of time. If the newsgroup is particularly active, articles might "scroll off" within a matter of days. Fortunately, there is a Web site devoted to the archiving of newsgroup articles. You can search the DejaNews site by newsgroup, by topic, or by author to find an article that no longer appears in a newsgroup.

1 Use your Web browser to go to the DejaNews main page, located at the following address:

http://www.dejanews.com

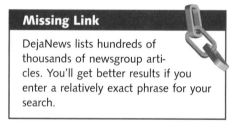

2 To search for a specific topic or user, enter a phrase to search for in the **Quick Search For:** box and click the **Find** button.

Missing Link

DejaNews lists hundreds of thousands of newsgroup articles. You'll get better results if you enter a relatively exact phrase for your search.

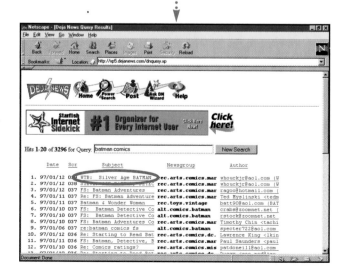

3 DejaNews returns a list of articles in various newsgroups that contain your search phrase. Click any article to view its contents.

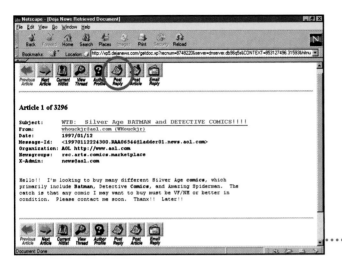

4 DejaNews displays the article itself. To reply to the article, click the **Post Reply** button.

> **Puzzled?**
>
> If the article is past a certain age, DejaNews will inform you that you can't reply to it.

5 When the Posting Service page appears, scroll down and enter your personal information, as well as the text of your reply. Click the **Check Your Posting** button to display your reply on a new page. When you finish, click the **Looks OKAY!** button to post the article.

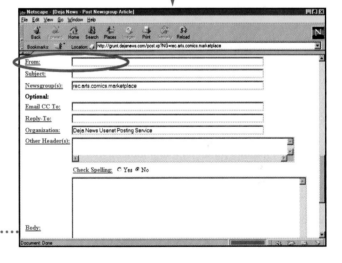

6 You can also use DejaNews to look for other articles from a particular author of newsgroup articles. On the Article page, click the **Author Profile** button to display a summary of articles posted to various groups by the author of the currently displayed article.

PART XI

Three Things to Know About Downloading Files

THE INTERNET IS A HUGE REPOSITORY for computer files of all shapes and sizes. There are tens of thousands of utilities and programs available *somewhere* on the Internet; if you can find them, you can download them to your computer.

Some of the files are actual computer programs; others are graphics files, text files, or documents for popular word processors or spreadsheets. Many users are especially interested in graphics files. The Internet is a great place to find clip art and images to use when you create your own Web page. (See Task 50 for more information on creating your own Web page.)

Of the program files available on the Net, many are available free of charge; that's called *freeware*. Other programs can be downloaded for no charge but require you to pay a token to receive full functionality or documentation; that's called *shareware*. Don't confuse either of these downloadable program types with the type you buy in a box at a retail store; that's commercial software, and you won't find much of it on the Internet.

There are three ways to download files from the Internet:

- **From a World Wide Web site.** Most files on the Internet are available from World Wide Web sites. In fact, several big sites have been created to help users find all the files available on the Web. One of the most popular of these sites is Download.com from the folks at c|net. Download.com doesn't actually store any files on its own site; you use Download.com to find files that are stored elsewhere on the Web. Then, using your Web browser, you can download those files with a click of your mouse.

- **From an FTP server.** If you know exactly where a file is located—on what server, and in what directory—it's sometimes faster to just download the file directly, bypassing any Web sites in-between. This direct download method is called *File Transfer Protocol*, or FTP for short. While you can find separate FTP programs, it's just as easy to use your Web browser to "ftp" files from the Net.

- **From a Gopher server.** In years past, many sites organized their files using a protocol called Gopher. Gopher was easier to use than FTP because it created an easily-navigable hierarchy of directories and subdirectories. However, in recent years the Web has supplanted Gopher as the preferred front end for file downloading, so there aren't a lot of Gopher-only servers available these days. The one place you're likely to run into a Gopher server, however, is on a university's site. While you can use a separate Gopher program, you can also can access Gopher servers using your Web browser.

Once you have downloaded a file to your hard disk, you can do something with it. If it's a program file, you probably have to install it to make it work. Many program files are large and are, therefore, *compressed* in some way to shorten downloading time. You may have to *decompress* a downloaded file before you can install it; many installation routines decompress files automatically.

One of the more popular compression/decompression standards is called ZIP; you *ZIP* your files to compress them, and you *UNZIP* compressed files. You can find several utilities to decompress ZIP files at Download.com (**http://www.download.com**). In particular, look for programs like PKZIP and WinZIP.

Obviously, file downloading is only good for those of you accessing the Internet through your personal computers. If you're a WebTV user, you should probably skip this section.

Downloading Files from the World Wide Web

"Why would I do this?"

Many specialty software programs and utilities just aren't available in your local software retail store. The only place to find many of these programs is on the Internet. Downloading these types of programs has become so popular that many Web sites have been created just to deal with file downloading. (Que even has its own software downloading site, located at **http://www.mcp.com/que/software/**.) Download.com, from c|net, is a good site to start with because it catalogs files found on other sites all around the world.

1 Go to the Download.com home page at the following address:**http://www. download. com**. Then click **Categories** to see a list of file categories.

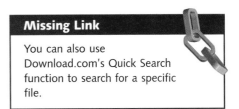

Missing Link

You can also use Download.com's Quick Search function to search for a specific file.

2 When the Categories list appears, click the desired category, such as **Internet**.

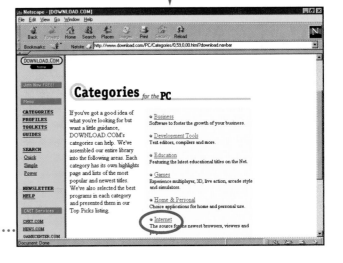

3 Choose a subcategory (such as **Chat**) and click it.

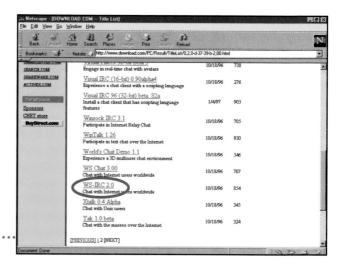

4 You'll see a list of all relevant files available for downloading. Click a file name to display more details.

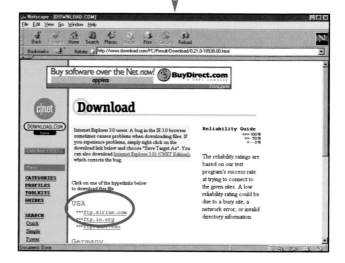

5 Read all about the selected file. If you want to download the file, click the **Click Here to Download** button.

6 When the Download page appears, select the site from which you want to download the file. If possible, try to choose a site near you; this minimizes Internet traffic and transmission time.

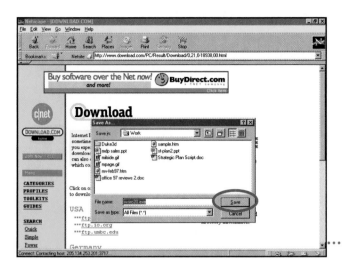

7 When the Save As dialog box appears, select the location where you want to save the file, and then click **Save**.

8 The Saving Location box shows the progress of your file download. When the file is completely downloaded and saved to your hard disk, this dialog box disappears. ■

Missing Link

After the file is downloaded, you can initiate its installation routine. Many files install themselves when you run the downloaded file; others require the use of an "unzip" program. Read the instructions at Download.com for details on how to install individual files.

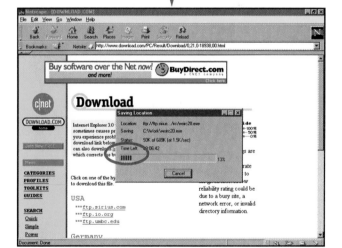

TASK 65

Downloading Files with FTP

"Why would I do this?"

Before the World Wide Web ever existed, files on the Internet were only accessible by means of a process called File Transfer Protocol, or FTP. Even today, many sites still store their files on FTP servers and merely include links to these FTP sites on easier-to-navigate Web pages. For that reason, it's sometimes faster to download files directly from an FTP site. This task shows you how to use your Web browser to download files stored on FTP servers.

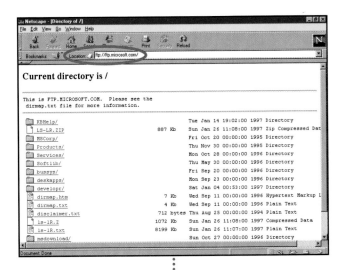

1 Enter the FTP address in Navigator's **Go to:** text box. For example, enter **ftp://ftp.microsoft.com** to go to Microsoft's FTP site.

Missing Link

To search among a variety of FTP sites for specific files, go to **http://www-ns.rutgers.edu/ htbin/archie**.

2 You'll see a list of directories and subdirectories with file icons next to them. Click a directory to view its contents.

Missing Link

When you access an FTP site, look for the **pub** directory. On many sites, the publicly accessible files are stored in a directory called pub.

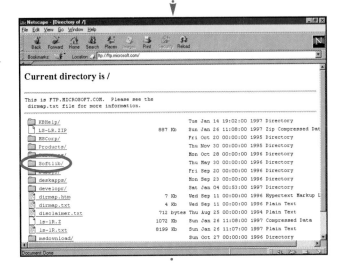

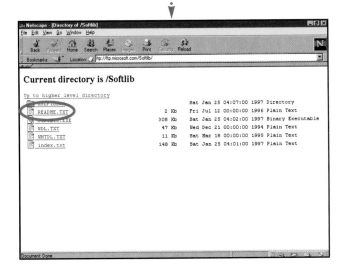

3 Click a specific file to view it or download it. ■

Puzzled?

If you click a text file, it automatically appears in your browser window for immediate viewing. If you click any other kind of file, the downloading procedure automatically begins.

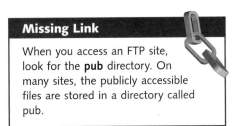

Downloading Files with Gopher

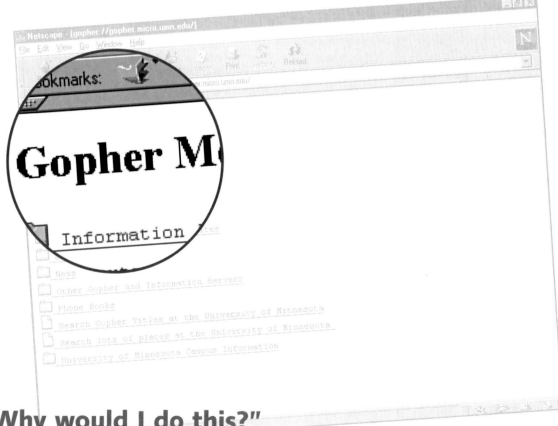

"Why would I do this?"

Between the original FTP and the advent of the World Wide Web, there was Gopher. Gopher was an attempt to organize files in a way that was easier to browse than a typical FTP server, using hierarchical directories and subdirectories in a folders-type metaphor (much like the directory listing used in Windows Explorer of Windows 95). If you're trying to find files on a university Internet site, chances are you'll run into a Gopher server; many universities invested heavily in Gopher and are only slowly moving their files to the World Wide Web. This task shows you how to navigate Gopher servers and download files using your Web browser.

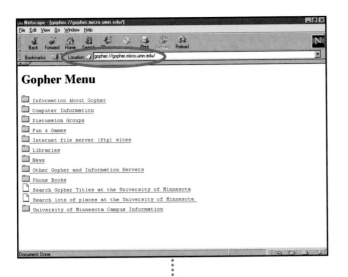

1 Enter the Gopher address in Navigator's **Go to:** text box. For example, enter **gopher://gopher.micro.umn.edu** to go to the Gopher site at the University of Minnesota—where the Gopher protocol was created!

Missing Link

Some people will tell you that Gopher got its name from the University of Minnesota mascot—the Golden Gopher; others will tell you it has to do with "burrowing" for information on the Internet. Believe what you will.

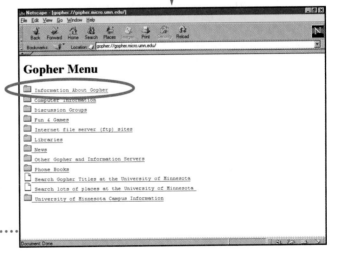

2 A gopher directory listing appears; it looks a lot like an FTP directory listing. Click a folder to see the contents of a directory or subdirectory.

3 When you find a file you want, click it to view it or download it. ■

PART XII

Three Things to Know About Chatting on the Net

INTERNET CHAT (ALSO CALLED Internet Relay Chat, or IRC for short) is kind of like one of those 900-number telephone chat lines—except you use your keyboard instead of a telephone, and you don't run up bills at $1.99/minute or more. When you enter a Chat "channel," you can just listen to conversations, or you can join in yourself. And you don't have to use your real name (you use a "nickname" instead), so you can remain as anonymous as you want to be.

There are dozens of different sites on the Internet that operate Chat *servers*. (A server is just a fancy name for a computer hooked up to the network of computers we call the Internet.)

You use a dedicated Chat program to access a Chat server over your normal Internet connection.

Once you're connected to a Chat server, you need to enter a Chat channel to begin your chat. Most servers offer dozens, if not hundreds, of channels, kind of like the channels on CB radios. Each channel is assigned a specific topic, so find a channel specializing in a topic you're interested in. Then start chatting!

Here are some tips to get you started chatting as painlessly as possible:

- Don't give out your real name, address, or phone number in a Chat channel—period.

- Don't assume you're talking to the person you think you're talking to. It's pretty easy to hide behind a nickname and create a totally different persona.

- If you want to get personal with someone you meet in a Chat channel, use the personal message feature of your Chat program. Don't subject everyone in a channel to your private conversations.

- Watch out for your kids. The online world is part of the real world, and Chat channels are good places for unsavory sorts to harass unknowing youngsters. Make sure that your kids are well informed, that they use good judgment, and that they never, *ever* arrange to meet a chatmate without your supervision.

- Spelling and grammar really don't count for much in Chat sessions, but try to at least make your messages understandable. It's also okay to abbreviate in Chat sessions; acronyms work just fine here, IMHO. (That's short for "in my humble opinion.")

The following list contains some of the most popular acronyms you'll find used in Internet Chat sessions.

Acronym	Meaning
AKA	Also known as
ASAP	As soon as possible
BTW	By the way
FWIW	For what it's worth
FYI	For your information
GD&R	Grinning, ducking, and running
IMHO	In my humble opinion
IOW	In other words
LOL	Laughing out loud
OTOH	On the other hand
PMJI	Pardon me for jumping in
ROFL	Rolling on the floor laughing
TLA	Three letter acronym
TTFN	Ta ta for now!

You can learn more about Internet Chat at the #IRChelp Web site, located at **http://www.irchelp.org.** This site not only provides information about Internet Chat, but also includes lists of all available Chat servers on the Internet. You can even find many of the most popular Chat programs available for downloading at the #IRChelp site.

Note that the only way to access Internet Chat is through an Internet Service Provider. Although they do not offer access to Internet Chat, America Online and CompuServe do have their own proprietary chat areas that serve much the same function. At this point in time, however, WebTV does not offer access to Chat servers.

Preparing for a Chat Session

"Why would I do this?"

When trading messages in a UseNet newsgroup isn't immediate enough, it's time to get involved with something called Internet Chat. Chat lets you communicate in real time with other users by connecting Chat servers on the Internet. You access Chat servers with a special Chat program, such as WS-IRC. (You can download a copy of WS-IRC from Que's Software Library, located at **http://www.mcp.com/que/software/isoftwre.html**.)

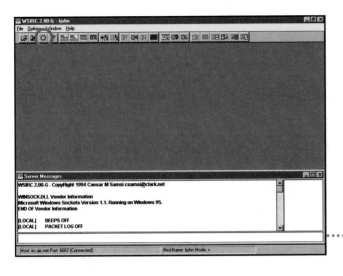

1 When you first launch WS-IRC you're prompted to complete some initial configuration settings. You can also do this manually by clicking the **Server Options Setup** button. The WS-IRC Server Options dialog box appears.

2 Enter the name of the IRC server to which you want to connect, its port number, the nickname you want to use, your user name (generally your real name), your e-mail address, and the name of your PC (also generally your real name). When you finish, click **OK**.

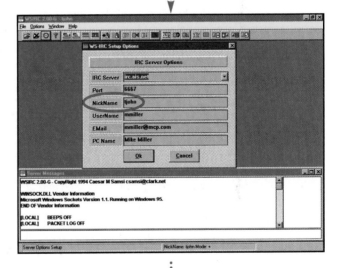

Missing Link

Go to **http:// www.irchelp. org/irchelp/ network.html** to find a list of hundreds of Chat servers. Choose a server geographically near you, if that's possible.

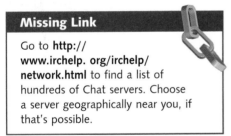

3 Click the **Connect To Server** button to connect to the IRC server you specified.

Puzzled?

If you get a message that the server is busy, either try connecting at a later time or change servers (via the Server Options dialog box).

4 When you're successfully connected, you'll see a welcome message in the Server Messages window. If you're ready to take part in a Chat conversation, see Task 68 for instructions.

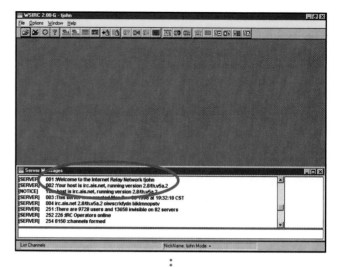

Puzzled?

If you receive a message that someone else with the same nick-name is already on this server, go back to the Server Options dialog box, change the name in the **Nick-Name** text box, and then reconnect.

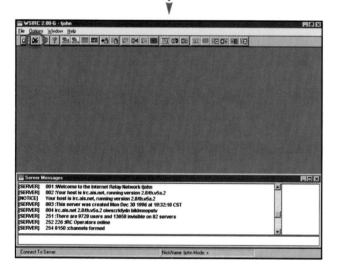

5 When you want to end your chat session, click the **Disconnect from Server** button. ■

Participating in Internet Chat

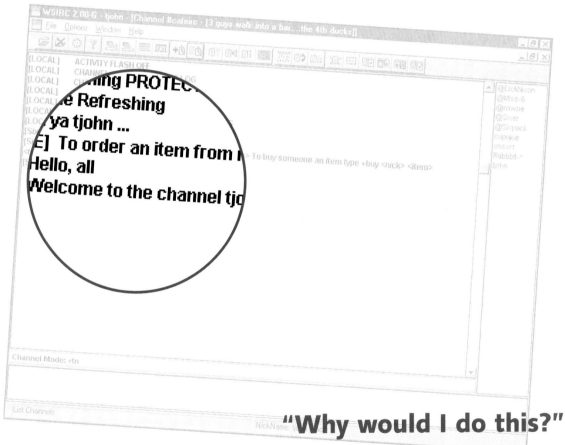

"Why would I do this?"

Each Chat server is a host to dozens of different channels. A *channel* is like a little online room devoted to a specific topic. You enter a channel to converse with other Chat users in real time, using your computer keyboard. Once you're connected to a Chat server, you can choose a channel and start chatting!

1 Connect to a Chat server (as you learned in Task 67), and then choose a channel to enter. To display a list of channels on this server, click the **List Channels** button.

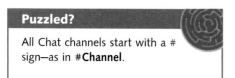

Puzzled?

All Chat channels start with a # sign—as in #**Channel**.

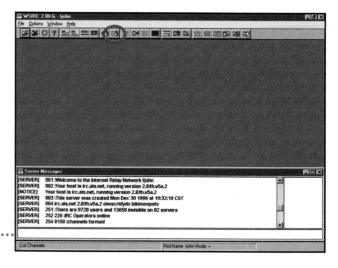

2 A list of the channels on this server appears in the right pane of the Server Messages window, along with the number of users currently participating in each channel. Double-click an entry to enter that channel.

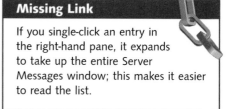

Missing Link

If you single-click an entry in the right-hand pane, it expands to take up the entire Server Messages window; this makes it easier to read the list.

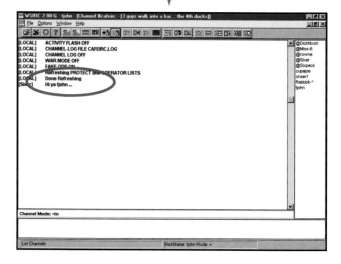

3 When you enter a channel, a new channel window appears. Chat messages are shown in the large pane. Current users in this channel are listed in a narrow pane on the right, and you enter your messages in the bottom pane.

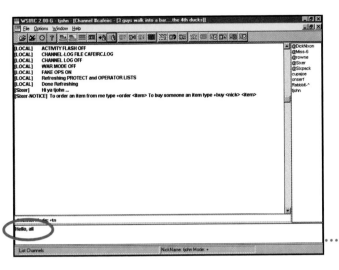

4 Enter a one-line message in the bottom pane.

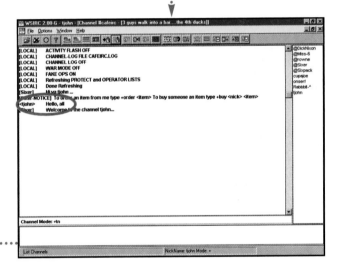

5 Press **Enter** to post the message to the Chat channel. Your message appears in the list of Chat messages almost immediately.

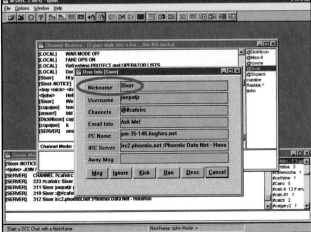

6 To find out more about another user in this channel, double-click the user's name in the user pane. A User Info dialog box appears, listing any information the person has included about himself.

Puzzled?

If no information shows up in the User Info dialog box, the user has not entered any personal information into his own IRC program.

221

7 If you prefer to send a private message to another user, click the **Send Private Message** button. A Private Message dialog box appears, with the user's nickname already entered. Enter your message *after* the nickname, and then click **OK** to send the message.

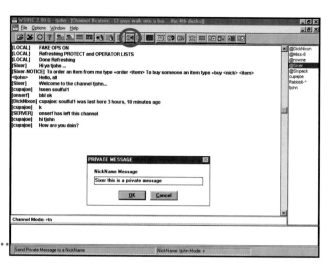

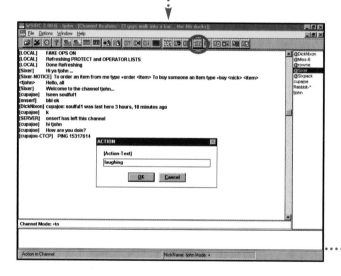

8 Sometimes you want to indicate to other users that you are performing an *action*, such as "Laughing" or "Leaving for a Minute." To do this, click the **Action** button, enter your action in the **[Action-Text]** box, and click **OK**. Your action shows up in the chat pane as a message with the header [ACTION].

9 To exit this channel, close the Channel window by double-clicking the window's **Close** (X) box. You can then open another channel or disconnect from this IRC server. ■

Puzzled?

Remember, even if you leave a channel, you're still connected to the IRC server until you manually disconnect; see Task 67 for details on disconnecting.

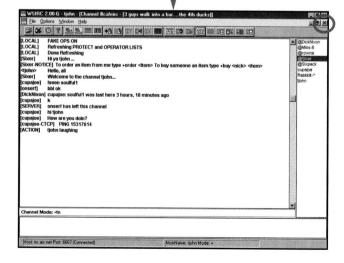

Using Microsoft Comic Chat

"Why would I do this?"

Microsoft has created a new type of Internet Chat, called Comic Chat. Unlike normal Chat, which is text-only, Comic Chat takes the messages floating around a Chat channel and uses them to create a continuous comic strip, with different cartoon characters representing the various Chat users. Aside from its cartoon aspect, Comic Chat operates pretty much like any other Chat program. You can download a copy of Comic Chat from **http://www.microsoft.com/ie/download/**.

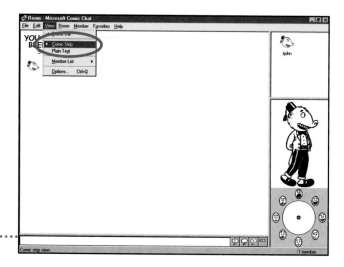

1 After you launch Comic Chat, you begin by setting a few options. First, make sure that you're viewing in comic strip mode (as opposed to text-only mode) by pulling down the **View** menu and selecting **Comic Strip**.

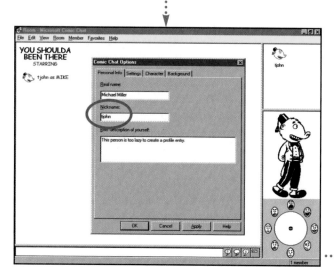

2 Now you can set your personal options. Pull down the **View** menu and select **Options**. Select the **Personal Info** tab and enter your real name, a nickname for yourself, and a brief description.

3 To select a character for yourself, click the **Character** tab. Choose one of the listed characters and click **OK**.

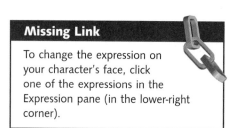

Missing Link

To change the expression on your character's face, click one of the expressions in the Expression pane (in the lower-right corner).

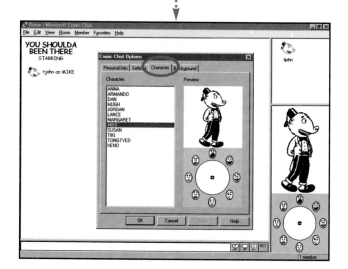

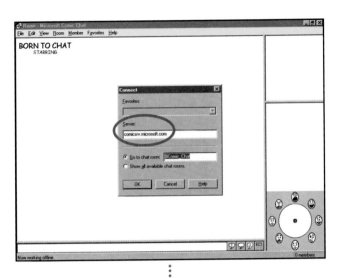

4 To connect to a Comic Chat server, pull down the **File** menu and select **New Connection**. When the Connect dialog box appears, enter the name of the server and click **OK**.

Missing Link

While Comic Chat works with any Chat server, users on a non-Comic Chat server won't be able to see your character—and the comic strip action might not always make sense. For best results, use Comic Chat on a Comic Chat server.

5 Choose a Chat room, and you see that other users are listed in the upper-right pane. Chat messages from other users are automatically transformed into a multi-paneled comic strip.

Missing Link

To view the user list as characters instead of plain text, pull down the **View** menu, select **Member List**, and choose **Icon**.

6 Enter your message in the bottom pane, and then click the **Say** button. Your character appears in the comic strip, saying your message. ■

Index

Symbols

* (asterisk), 93, 104, 183
$ (dollar sign), 96
- (minus sign), 92, 95, 100, 104
. (period), 96
+ (plus sign), 92, 100, 104, 191, 194
800 numbers, ISP, 19

A

acronyms, Internet, chatting, 215
Action button, 222
addresses
    e-mail, 174-175, 182-183
    searching, 106-109, 127
Advanced Query page, syntax, advanced, 105
airline reservations, making, 149-150
Alignment button, 170, 172
AllPolitics, CNN, 113
AltaVista, 10, 45
    Advanced Query page, advanced syntax, 105
    UseNet newsgroups, searching, 105
    WWW, searching, 102-105
AltaVista Web site, 79, 103
Amazon.com Web site, 146
America Online Web site, 19
America Online, see AOL
America's HouseCall Network Web site, 140-141
AOL (America Online), 14-15, 19, 22-23, 26
    e-mail, creating/reading, 42
    home page, Internet search, 40

Internet
    features, accessing, 39
    surfing, 38
UseNet newsgroups, accessing, 41
Web browser, accessing, 39
Web sites, accessing, 39
Archie Web site, 79
Arthur Frommer's Outspoken Encyclopedia of Travel Web site, 146
Article window, 200
articles
    newsgroups
        posting, 196-198
        reading, 51, 194-195
        responding to, 196-198
        selecting, 37
        threads, 188
        viewing, 41
    threads, reading, 193-195
    typeface, read/unread, 195
AT&T Web site, 19
Attach File button, 181
Author Profile button, 203
autosearch, Internet Explorer, Yahoo! version, 83

B

Background button, 169
BCC (Blind Carbon Copy), 181
Begin the Search button, 113
Berit's Best Sites for Children Web site, 131
Bess Web site, 17
Big Foot, search engine, 182-183
Big Foot Web site, 183
binary format, files, 199-200

bookmark lists
    editing, 73
    moving bookmarks, 74
    removing an item, 74
    selecting a bookmark, 73
    separators, inserting, 74
    subdividing, 75
Bookmark Properties dialog box, 75
bookmarks
    folders, adding to, 75
adding Web sites, 29
    in Netscape Navigator, 74
    shortcuts, copying, 75
    Web pages, 72-75
Bookmarks button, 29
Bookmarks command (Window menu), 73
Bookmarks menu, Netscape Navigator, 74
Britannica Online Web site, 131, 138-139
browsing, Web pages, 58-59
Bullet List button, 172
businesses, searching, 109
buttons
    Action, 222
    Alignment, 170, 172
    Attach File, 181
    Author Profile, 203
    Background, 169
    Begin the Search, 113
    Bookmarks, 29
    Bullet List, 172
    Check Your Posting, 203
    Click Here to Download, 208
    Compose, 181, 187
    Connect, 36
    Connect To Server, 217
    Delete, 177
    Disconnect from Server, 218
    Display on Desktop, 115

Index

Index

Inbox window, 35
information
    desktop, receiving, 147
    searching, 10
    Web sites, 110
Infoseek, 45
    Ultraseek, 98-101
    words, specific, searching, 100
Infoseek Web site, 79, 147
Insert Folder command (Item menu), 75
Insert Horz. Line button, 171
Insert Image button, 171
Insert Separator command (Item menu), 74
installing, files, 209
INTELLiCast Web site, 111
Internet
    AOL
        features, accessing, 39
        home page, searching, 40
        surfing, 38
    basics to know, 7
    chat sessions, 219-222
    chatting, 214-215
    CompuServe Interactive, 48-49
    connecting to, 9
    Internet Explorer, surfing, 33
    MSN, searching, 45
    news/information, narrowcast-
        ing, 164-167
    service providers, 19
    software, 26-27
    WebTV
        accessing, 25
        surfing, 53
Internet 101 Web site, 7
Internet Chat
    Comic Chat, 223-225
    sessions
        ending, 218
        preparing for, 216-218
Internet Explorer, 13, 27, 59
    Autosearch, Yahoo! version, 83
    e-mail messages, creating/
        reading, 35
    filtering capabilities, 17
    surfing, 33

UseNet newsgroups,
    accessing, 36
Web sites, accessing, 34
WWW, searching, 82-83
Internet Explorer commands
    Go menu
        Open History Folder, 71
    View menu
        Options, 69
Internet Health Resources Web site,
    131
Internet Mall, shopping, 152-155
Internet Mall Web site, 153-155
Internet Relay Chat, see IRC
Internet Service Provider, see ISP
Internet services, 18
Internet Shortcut, 75
Internet software, 13
investment information, Hoover's Web
    site, 120-121
IRC (Internet Relay Chat), 214-215
ISDN lines, 13
ISP (Internet Service Provider), 18
    800 numbers, 19
    accessing, 9
    accounts, 13, 15
    establishing connections, 21
    finding, 14
    local/national, comparing, 21
    online services, comparing, 15
    software, obligations, 15
    Web browsers, 27
    what to look for, 15
Item menu commands
    Insert Folder, 75
    Insert Separator, 74

J-K-L

job listings, corporate Web sites, 121
Join Discussion Group command (File
    menu), 31
keyboards, WebTV, 25
KidNews Web site, 131
KidsDoctor Web site, 131
KidSource Web site, 131
KidSpace Web site, 131, 134-135
lastname, e-mail, 187

launching, Netscape Navigator, 29
linking, hypertext links, 172
links, graphics/hypertext, 58
List Channels button, 220
list managers, e-mail, 174
listname, e-mail, 187
Location text box, 63
Looks OKAY! button, 203
Lycos, 94-97
Lycos City Guide Web site, 126
Lycos Web site, 95-97

M

M. Miller Web site, 175
Mail button, 35-36
mailing lists
    canceling, 187
    obtaining, 184-185
    special interests, 11
    subjects, sorted, 185
    subscribing to, 186-187
Make Link button, 172-173
MapQuest Web site, 146
MCI Internet Dial Access Web site, 19
Member List command (View menu),
    225
Message Center window, 32
messages
    e-mail, reading, 42
    newsgroups, 32, 37
    WebTV e-mail, composing/
        reading, 57
Microsoft Internet Explorer, 26
Microsoft Network Web site, 19, 147
Microsoft Network, see MSN
Microsoft Web site, 26
Microsoft's FTP site, 211
Microsoft's Internet Explorer, 6, 33
minus sign (-), 92, 95, 100, 104
modems, 13
    ISP, accessing, 9
    Web pages, browsing, 59
monitors, color, 13
More Results button, 85
Move Down button, 166
Move Up button, 166
Mr. Showbiz Web site, 111, 124-125

Index

Parents Place Web site, 131
ParentTime Web site, 131
PC (Personal Computer), Pentium based, 13
Pentium, PC, 13
people, cities, searching, 127
period (.), 96
personal computer, *see* PC
Personal Seek Web site, 79, 147
Personalize button, 166
plus sign (+), 92, 100, 104, 191, 194
PointCast, screen saver, 167
PointCast Network, narrowcasting, 164-167
PointCast Web site, 165-167
Post Message button, 37
Post Reply button, 203
Preferences command (Netscape Navigator, Edit menu), 69
Preferences dialog box, 69
Print button, 77
Print dialog box, 77
printing, Web pages, 76-77
Private Message dialog box, 222
Prodigy Internet, 23
Prodigy Internet Web site, 19
program, files
    compressed, ZIP, 205
    decompressed, UNZIP, 205
programs, files, freeware, 204
Properties dialog box, 171-173
protecting, children, 16-17
protocols, ISDN lines, 13
Publicly Accessible Mailing Lists Web site, 185

Q-R

Que Web site, 27, 206, 216
Quick Search function, 207
Quick Seek function, 153
Quote Original button, 179, 197
QuoteCom Web site, 111

Re:Mail button, 179
Re:News button, 197
Read My Newsgroups icon, 41
Read New Mail icon, 42

Receive button, 35
Refresh button, 34
Reload button, 65
remote controls, WebTV, 25
Reply button, 30, 32, 179
Reply to Author button, 35, 47
Reply to Group button, 37
road maps, 127

S

Satellite Image button, 167
Save As command (File menu), 77
Save As command (Netscape Composer, File menu), 169
Save As dialog box, 200, 209
Save button, 173
saving
    files, pictures, 199-200
    Web pages, 40, 77
Saving Location dialog box, 209
Say button, 225
screen savers, PointCast, 167
screens, Flight Search, 149
Search button, 91, 183
search engines, 45
    AltaVista, 10, 102-105
    Big Foot, 182-183
    Excite, 84-85
    Lycos, 94-97
    Search.com, locating, 86-89
    Switchboard, 106-109
    Ultraseek, 98
        activating, 101
    Web pages, 78
    Yahoo!, 10, 83
Search icon, 85
Search New button, 191
search sites, 79
Search Yahoo! button, 83
Search.com
    search engines, locating, 86-89
    WWW, searching, 86-89
Search.com Web site, 79, 87
searching, information, 10
secure server, 155
security, credit transactions, 155
Send button, 30, 35, 179

Send Private Message button, 222
Server Messages window, 220
Server Options dialog box, 217
Server Options Setup button, 217
service providers
    America Online, 19
    AT&T WorldNet, 19
    CompuServe Interactive, 19
    GTE Internet Solutions, 19
    MCI Internet Dial Access, 19
    Microsoft Network, 19
    Netcom, 19
    Prodigy Internet, 19
    Sprint Internet Passport, 19
    Web TV, 19
Settings button, 17
Seussville (Dr. Seuss) Web site, 131
shareware, programs, files, 204
shopping
    credit transactions, secure, 155
    WWW, 146
        Internet Mall, 152-155
shortcuts
    bookmarks, copying, 75
    Internet Shortcut, 75
sites
    FTP
        Microsoft, 211
    Gopher
        University of Minnesota, 213
    Web *see* Web sites
snail mail, 174
soap operas, updates, TV Guide Online Web site, 123
software
    AOL, 26
    CompuServe Interactive, 27
    filtering, SurfWatch, 130
    filtering, Web sites, 130
    Internet, 13, 26-27
    ISP, 15, 18
    kid safe
        Cyber Patrol, 17
        CYBERsitter, 17
        Net Nanny, 17
        programs, 16
        SurfWatch, 17
    Lycos, spider, 94-97

Index

Complete and Return this Card for a *FREE* Computer Book Catalog

Thank you for purchasing this book! You have purchased a superior computer book written expressly for your needs. To continue to provide the kind of up-to-date, pertinent coverage you've come to expect from us, we need to hear from you. Please take a minute to complete and return this self-addressed, postage-paid form. In return, we'll send you a free catalog of all our computer books on topics ranging from word processing to programming and the internet.

Mr. ☐   Mrs. ☐   Ms. ☐   Dr. ☐

Name (first) ☐☐☐☐☐☐☐☐☐☐☐   (M.I.) ☐   (last) ☐☐☐☐☐☐☐☐☐☐☐☐☐☐☐☐

Address ☐☐☐☐☐☐☐☐☐☐☐☐☐☐☐☐☐☐☐☐☐☐☐☐☐☐☐☐☐☐☐

☐☐☐☐☐☐☐☐☐☐☐☐☐☐☐☐☐☐☐☐☐☐☐☐☐☐☐☐☐☐☐

City ☐☐☐☐☐☐☐☐☐☐☐   State ☐☐   Zip ☐☐☐☐☐ ☐☐☐☐

Phone ☐☐☐ ☐☐☐ ☐☐☐☐   Fax ☐☐☐ ☐☐☐ ☐☐☐☐

Company Name ☐☐☐☐☐☐☐☐☐☐☐☐☐☐☐☐☐☐☐☐☐☐☐☐☐☐☐☐☐☐

E-mail address ☐☐☐☐☐☐☐☐☐☐☐☐☐☐☐☐☐☐☐☐☐☐☐☐☐☐☐☐

1. Please check at least (3) influencing factors for purchasing this book.

Front or back cover information on book .... ☐
Special approach to the content .... ☐
Completeness of content .... ☐
Author's reputation .... ☐
Publisher's reputation .... ☐
Book cover design or layout .... ☐
Index or table of contents of book .... ☐
Price of book .... ☐
Special effects, graphics, illustrations .... ☐
Other (Please specify): _____

2. How did you first learn about this book?

Saw in Macmillan Computer Publishing catalog .... ☐
Recommended by store personnel .... ☐
Saw the book on bookshelf at store .... ☐
Recommended by a friend .... ☐
Received advertisement in the mail .... ☐
Saw an advertisement in: _____ ☐
Read book review in: _____ ☐
Other (Please specify): _____ ☐

3. How many computer books have you purchased in the last six months?

This book only .... ☐   3 to 5 books .... ☐
2 books .... ☐   More than 5 .... ☐

4. Where did you purchase this book?

Bookstore .... ☐
Computer Store .... ☐
Consumer Electronics Store .... ☐
Department Store .... ☐
Office Club .... ☐
Warehouse Club .... ☐
Mail Order .... ☐
Direct from Publisher .... ☐
Internet site .... ☐
Other (Please specify): _____ ☐

5. How long have you been using a computer?

☐ Less than 6 months   ☐ 6 months to a year
☐ 1 to 3 years   ☐ More than 3 years

6. What is your level of experience with personal computers and with the subject of this book?

	With PCs	With subject of book
New	☐	☐
Casual	☐	☐
Accomplished	☐	☐
Expert	☐	☐

Source Code ISBN: 0-7897-1219-9

7. Which of the following best describes your job title?

Administrative Assistant .... ☐
Coordinator .... ☐
Manager/Supervisor .... ☐
Director .... ☐
Vice President .... ☐
President/CEO/COO .... ☐
Lawyer/Doctor/Medical Professional ...... ☐
Teacher/Educator/Trainer .... ☐
Engineer/Technician .... ☐
Consultant .... ☐
Not employed/Student/Retired .... ☐
Other (Please specify): _____ ☐

8. Which of the following best describes the area of the company your job title falls under?

Accounting .... ☐
Engineering .... ☐
Manufacturing .... ☐
Operations .... ☐
Marketing .... ☐
Sales .... ☐
Other (Please specify): _____ ☐

9. What is your age?

Under 20 .... ☐
21-29 .... ☐
30-39 .... ☐
40-49 .... ☐
50-59 .... ☐
60-over .... ☐

10. Are you:

Male .... ☐
Female .... ☐

11. Which computer publications do you read regularly? (Please list)

_____
_____
_____
_____
_____
_____
_____
_____
_____

Comments: _____
_____
_____

Fold here and scotch-tape to mail.

Check out Que® Books on the World Wide Web
http://www.mcp.com/que

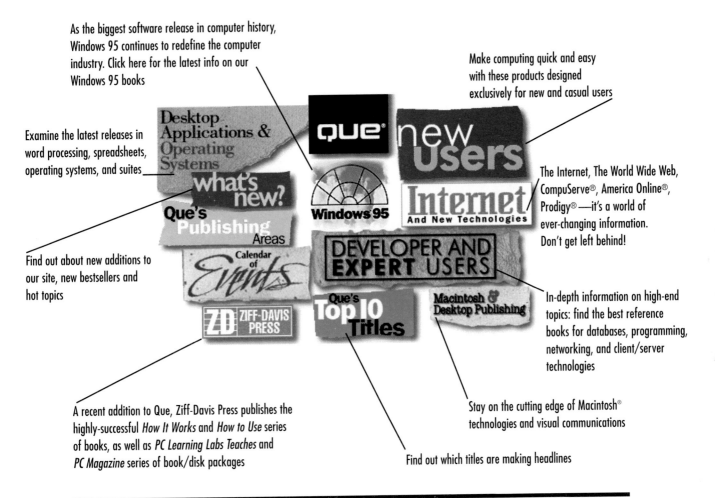

As the biggest software release in computer history, Windows 95 continues to redefine the computer industry. Click here for the latest info on our Windows 95 books

Examine the latest releases in word processing, spreadsheets, operating systems, and suites

Find out about new additions to our site, new bestsellers and hot topics

Make computing quick and easy with these products designed exclusively for new and casual users

The Internet, The World Wide Web, CompuServe®, America Online®, Prodigy® —it's a world of ever-changing information. Don't get left behind!

In-depth information on high-end topics: find the best reference books for databases, programming, networking, and client/server technologies

A recent addition to Que, Ziff-Davis Press publishes the highly-successful *How It Works* and *How to Use* series of books, as well as *PC Learning Labs Teaches* and *PC Magazine* series of book/disk packages

Stay on the cutting edge of Macintosh® technologies and visual communications

Find out which titles are making headlines

With 6 separate publishing groups, Que develops products for many specific market segments and areas of computer technology. Explore our Web Site and you'll find information on best-selling titles, newly published titles, upcoming products, authors, and much more.

- Stay informed on the latest industry trends and products available
- Visit our online bookstore for the latest information and editions
- Download software from Que's library of the best shareware and freeware

MACMILLAN COMPUTER PUBLISHING USA

A VIACOM COMPANY

Technical ---- Support:

If you need assistance with the information in this book or with a CD/Disk accompanying the book, please access the Knowledge Base on our Web site at **http://www.superlibrary.com/general/support**. Our most Frequently Asked Questions are answered there. If you do not find the answer to your questions on our Web site, you may contact Macmillan Technical Support **(317) 581-3833** or e-mail us at **support@mcp.com**.